*I was given a second chance to do whatever I wanted to
do with my life and that's exactly what I did.*

I grew up as a gang member on the streets of New York City, and I retired from the Nassau County Police Department, having reached the rank of a three-star division chief, the second-highest uniformed position in the 3,500 member department. I had 700 officers working for me. I'm a lawyer now, but as a kid, I sampled a wide variety of drugs. I stayed high on weed from morning till night. I stole drugs, and I sold drugs. I did robberies, burglaries, pocketbook snatches, assaults—you name it! Some of my friends grew up to be killers. I lived in a roach-infested tenement apartment building, and I was the only white kid in the gang. Everybody else was Hispanic or black. I learned about sex on top of an apartment house with a girl called "Rooftop Rosie." Now I'm paid a six-figure pension just for waking up in the morning. And I make a lot more than that from my business ventures. Most of the other kids in my crew are dead, crippled, or doing hard time. I got shot, locked up, beat up, and robbed; and I robbed and beat up other kids. It was a rush! And it was a horrible existence that almost ruined my life.

My father was a drunk and my mother was a pill head. I loved them both but I couldn't stand being around them. They loved me too, but they couldn't see me because they were busy fighting violently from dusk to dawn. They wallowed in their own misery and they had no time to look after me. I guess they thought I was okay. They just couldn't see where I was going. I escaped to be with a group of boys who had it worse than I did. The street beckoned with solace, family, and adventure. I longed to be black. I dressed black. I walked black and I talked black. I dated only black girls. But I was white. That was my identity crisis, and it fucked up my self-esteem.

From the streets, I learned firsthand about racism. And I'm not talking about the kind of racism that is measured by political correctness. I have experienced hardcore, genuine, and sometimes violent hatred from whites and blacks alike. That's real racism! Every time the gang got into a confrontation with a group of white kids, I was the first one to get hit. Whenever the cops rolled upon us, and it happened a lot, I was the first one with his face against the bricks. My parents wouldn't allow any racist words to be used in our home. In the streets, they called me nigger lover, wannabe, peckerwood, and cracker. Back in the lair, the brothers broke my white balls relentlessly, but in a half-joking way that creates a pain that you feel much later. When we went out of our turf, they would, at times, have to protect me from the blacks outside of our crew who didn't know me but hated me just because I was white. I did my best to pass for Puerto Rican when I could. And when the 'Five Percenter' movement hit, they told me that the black man was God, and the white man was the devil. I started believing it. That's where my head was at that time.

I have two children now, an amazing wife, and by all accounts, I am a wealthy man. I worry every day that my son is too much like me. I didn't want him to read this book while he was in his vulnerable and impressionable adolescence. I am an enigma. Most kids never climb out of the hole I dug when I was a teen, but I couldn't expect him to realize that.

Regrets? I have a few, but fewer to mention. I have a life that others envy, and I owe it to the sum of my experiences. As a decorated beat cop, I called on those experiences to keep myself one step ahead of the bad guys. What almost killed me as a boy saved my life more than once as a man. I knew what the criminals were going to do because I had been a criminal. *Thief to Chief* is my story.

DON'T JUDGE ME

BY MY PAST,

I DON'T LIVE THERE

ANYMORE.

FROM
THIEF
TO
CHIEF

A SELF-PORTRAIT
OF JUVENILE DELINQUENCY
AND REHABILITATION

KEVIN LOWRY

ISBN: 978-1-09832-397-4

TABLE OF CONTENTS

ACKNOWLEDGMENT

Several people have played pivotal roles in my life, and most of them don't even know it. I am eternally grateful to them for their contributions. Hopefully, they will somehow learn through the pages of my story, the tremendous influence they have had on me.

First is the Nassau County Police Department, and perhaps more significantly, Sgt. Boylan from the Applicant Investigation Unit. Sgt. Boylan knew some things about my history which could have disqualified me as a candidate for the job. Yet, she weighed the progress I had made by then against my past and decided to take a chance on me. She advocated my position, and I did not let her down. Then the department gave me twenty-eight years of a tremendously fulfilling and exciting career, teaching me compassion, leadership, and how to run a business.

Next is Chenee Gardenhire, a former girlfriend of mine, and Mr. Ed West, my probation officer. You will read about them in the pages to come. They both came into my life at a critical juncture and helped me cheat the devil by restoring in me the confidence to change my fate.

Third, are my wife's parents Rita and Vinny. They had their doubts about me when we first met, and I had no job, but they soon loved me like their own son. They are simply the most generous and compassionate people I have ever known. When they had nothing, they would always find a way to help those in need. And Mama Rita who, after raising five daughters with two still living in their humble three-bedroom home, went back to night school for her college degree. She alone inspired me to go to law school.

Finally, I acknowledge my parents Mimi and Semmes. Despite their own personal problems, they loved me dearly, and they instilled in me the values that echoed in my mind even during my darkest hours. They were the angels on my shoulder, always nudging me toward a respectable law-abiding life of service toward God and man. In my formative years, my mother and father carefully constructed my personality on a foundation of confidence and instilled in me a "can do" attitude. Those lessons were there, under the surface, desperately trying to erupt all those years when I felt worthless. Thank God, I finally hit the relief valve. I have showered my own children with the same love and I have never allowed them to say "I can't." That is my lasting tribute to my mom and dad.

DEDICATION

As I write this, I am sixty years old. Life has passed quickly. Back in Flushing, sixty years could have been a thousand. That's how it is for a teenager; nothing matters except today. Now, I often contemplate death. I'm not afraid to die. I do feel sorry for those who will mourn me, but I've had a good life. What I fear most is the possibility that my wife may go before me. The thought of going on without her frightens me tremendously. She is the most precious part of my life. Annie is my confidant, my lover, my business partner, and my closest friend. All of the joy in my life has her fingerprints on it. She has brought to me all the blessings that a man could desire; our glorious children Mackenzie and Rudd, a wonderful home, encouragement, practicality, unwavering support, and love that grows deeper every day. Wife, mother, baker, artist, lover, planner, cook, CFO; together, we march through life arm in arm. No obstacle is too great when we face it together. There can be no question then that this book, and indeed every breath I take, is dedicated to my forever valentine, my wife, Annie Lowry.

PROLOGUE

I sure as hell wasn't going to kill anybody. This was a tight spot.

It was dreary and dank in the carriage room, deep in the catacombs of my apartment building. Gone were the days when mothers kept their kids' strollers and bikes in there. Nobody stored anything in there anymore because it wasn't safe. People rarely came through that part of the basement at all anymore, especially at night. The laundry room was under building two. That was the side of the building I lived on. Our storage room/clubhouse was under building one. The two buildings were connected by a tunnel, but there really wasn't any need for most people to pass through there. You could walk around the outside if you needed to get to the back of the building. Tenants used to use the labyrinth as a passageway to the courtyard that led to the garage in building three. Few people kept their cars in the garage anymore because it was frightening going down there alone in that neighborhood. Though the truth is that it was a lot safer in those places than most other places around town. That was our turf, and we hung out in those spots, but we respected our neighbors. We would steal anything left behind, but we wouldn't rob anybody who lived there and we wouldn't break into their cars. Nobody else would either, knowing that we stood guard. I can see how the people in that complex were probably afraid of us too. After all, that's really how we wanted it to be; how we needed it to be. All the time.

A single bare light bulb swung from the ceiling, dangling between some heating pipes caked in crumbling insulation. Hindsight hints that it was probably asbestos. Who knew?

The mood was somber. Somebody jumped Robazz and Kasseem's cousin. The Family was on high alert. We had no clue who did it. Nevertheless, it was surely the work of rival gang members. The boys from The Hill had crossed the line and there would be payback. I don't think any of us really believed that The Hill had anything to do with the beating, but that didn't matter to Kasseem and Robazz. Their cousin was in the hospital and some-body was going to suffer their vengeance. They needed someone to blame.

A pudgy brown, winged water bug bolted across the cement as the door swung in. Water bugs were giant cockroaches, and they thrived down there in that basement. Ballah used to catch them and paint numbers on their backs with a little paintbrush and a tube of paint he had stashed in the top drawer of the old dresser in the corner. He must have missed this one. The gang had been holed up in that room for about three hours, waiting for Robazz and Kasseem. We were probably stoned. The morning started with a wake and bake, and it went on all day.

"Why don't y'all give your minds a rest?" Robazz's mother used to say.

We didn't listen. Finally, the two brothers burst into the room. Robazz spoke as Kasseem laid six pistols on the floor, one for each of us. Their afros were soaked and beads of rain rolled off the tops of their heads.

It must be raining pretty hard out there, I thought.

"Those white mother fuckahs wupped my cuz. Now we go to war."

The message was clear. Each of us was to pick up one of those guns. Refusal would have had dire consequences. Kasseem lit a joint, took two deep tokens, passed it to his brother and said, "Let's go."

That moment still haunts me. It wakes me up at night to this day. "Let's go." And we went.

I was a bad kid. I did it all: larceny, drug-dealing, vandalism, pocket-picking, burglary, and robbery. We all did. The crazy thing about it was that I didn't think I was a bad kid at the time. I never wanted to hurt anybody and I tried to avoid the rough stuff unless someone came after me or mine. For me, it was all about the excitement, being where the action was, and fitting in with the tough group. My crew had the respect of other boys in the neighborhood, even the older ones. I was oblivious to the pain my parents were going through, or maybe I just didn't care. They pretty much abandoned me when their fighting started. At least, that's how I saw it. In my mind, I was alone. I needed to find a new family and these guys suited me just fine. We were "The Family." Being the only white kid in the crowd also gave me some warped kind of celebrity status, but it gave me plenty of hard times too. There were psycho-social dynamics taking place that eluded my adolescent understanding. I would only come to grasp the true phenomenon many years later.

There were two stolen cars outside. One was an AMC Javelin and the other was a four-door Mercury Marquis. I sure as hell wasn't going to kill anybody. This was a tight spot. How was I going to get out of this one? I dragged myself into the back seat of the Mercury. I didn't have the status to ride shotgun and the back of that two-door Javelin seemed like a trap to me. I'd seen guys leap out of the front seats of cars like that, and slam the doors behind them when shit hit the fan. Some asshole would be left in the back, scrambling to escape or defend himself. Back seats were a trap. I knew better than to be that guy. We split up and went hunting for boys from The Hill. The sky was teaming and the streets were empty. A couple of police cars were huddled under an overhang in a drive-through bank. I didn't know it then, but that was a refuge I would take many times in my future.

My pulse was cranking. I could feel the pump of the vein in my neck. I could feel my aorta throbbing, and I needed to take a piss.

"We're not fuckin stopping!" Kasseem growled.

We drove on.

The hunting party cruised the steamy streets for hours, smoking reefer and saying very little. Rain slashed the windows as we moved slowly up one block and then down the next. Kasseem raged on about what he was going to do to "those cocksuckers when we catch them."

Heaven deliver me from the fate of this night, I thought.

There wasn't a Hill boy to be found. The weather had driven the unsuspecting young men underground. Of course, they were unsuspecting, they hadn't done anything. We called it off when the night sky began to lighten. Together, we reluctantly agreed to go out again the next night. My relief was indescribable. Immediately, I began scheming on a way to avoid the next day's foray. That afternoon the cops locked up two rival drug dealers for hospitalizing the brothers' cousin. No one from The Hill was involved. That's when I knew I had to get out.

Fighting fires in high-rise apartment houses, jumping twenty-foot cliffs on skis, and high-speed pursuits in my police car—that's how I got my kicks in mid-life. I was born to seek thrills. We were boys. Boys will be boys no matter where they grow up; if they grow up. Non-stop action–that's what they crave. There is no such thing as enough excitement. It's a constant competition for bragging rights. Who can do the craziest, stupidest shit and live to tell about it! Nothing is too outrageous or too dangerous to consider, and the less consideration the idea gets, the more likely it's going to get done. How much fun is it going to be and how long are people going to be talking about it when it's over? That's all that matters. Boys growing up in New York City have an unlimited source of adrenaline-jammed, semi-suicidal stunts to test the limits of their balls and their brains, in that order. It's all fun and games until somebody loses an eye. Or his freedom. Or his life!

A huge wooden billboard was erected one afternoon on an overgrown, garbage-strewn lot on the 41st Road. It read, "FUTURE SITE OF THE NEW BOYS' CLUB." That sign stood there for about three years without as much as a shovel full of dirt being turned. In the back of that lot stood the skeleton of a tall maple tree. Dangling from one of the arms of that skeleton was a hemp rope that was hung there by an unknown person or persons. Boys have a remarkable attraction to ropes. We like to hang on them. We like to throw them. We love to swing on them. We like tying them. And we love climbing them. Every neighborhood kid had done his best Tarzan act on that line, a time or two, but I envisioned greater possibilities. I had seen a program on television about Marine Corps training and rappelling. Now that looked like fun! My plan was to rappel from that branch, about fifteen feet up off the dirt. As one of my buddies stood by as witness, I set out to clamor up the trunk of that old tree and to slide out onto that branch. If not for the verbal encouragement of my loyal friend Allen, I probably would have given up once I reached the wobbly limb. But with the moral support of that kid on the ground, the occasional, "Aww man, you're a faggot," and the fear of the stories of cowardice that would get back to the street, I pressed on. I yanked my body up onto that ragged old branch and it began to bounce. Dragging myself, chest down on my belly along that limb, I finally reached the loop securing the old rope to the older tree. There, below me, dangled a thin strand of braided hemp. Let boot camp begin! I slid off the branch and, hanging there by both hands, came face to face with the rush I craved, short-lived as it would be. Typical twelve-year-old nonsense. As I took hold of it with my right hand, I instantly realized that it was far too skinny to shimmy down. I abruptly abandoned the plan.

"You're an asshole. You neva shudda done this," Allen observed.

Randy and Allen were a couple of nerdy sons of ultra-nerdy parents. Neither of the boys would ever do anything even remotely resembling ballsy. They got their rush from hanging out with other kids who did ballsy shit. This time, of course, Allen was quite right.

"Yeahh thanks a lot pussy. I'm gonna swing back up."

So that was Plan B. First, get both hands back on that tired limb. Next, swing my legs up and wrap them around the branch. Finally, pull myself back up on top, crawl back to the trunk, and climb down. Piece of cake. One swing. Two swings. "Cracko!" It was the branch that surrendered, not me.

The moment I hit the ground, I knew my arm was broken. It also turned out to be a dislocated shoulder. I wound up with a cast covering my entire torso with my right arm up in the air. The doctors called it the 'Statue of Liberty' position. I had that cast on for about six weeks. I had to wear my father's shirts to school. The teachers kept calling on me, thinking I was raising my hand. It was actually an asset on Halloween. I took a paper shopping bag filled with eggs and hung it from the casted arm. The problem was that I was right-handed. I had to kind of lob the missiles at their targets like hand grenades. It was effective on large objects like city busses, but against a mobile opponent, I had no chance.

Casts were made of plaster in the 60s. A fresh cast was like a brand-new train car on the D-subway line. It begged for graffiti. All my buddies signed on the cast and wrote interesting anecdotes on the front and back. One kid drew a set of tits on my chest. It used to itch like getting in the car after a day at the beach. I used a ruler to scratch where I could and I cut little holes in strategic spots giving me access to some otherwise unreachable itch zones.

Back at the lot, I lay there, face down in the dirt, while Allen ran for my mother. It seemed like he was gone a long time so I began to yell for help. Finally, an old black lady emerged from the house behind the lot. I helplessly explained my dilemma and asked her to call an ambulance. She stood there a while and didn't say anything. I couldn't see her from my position on the ground, but I sensed that she hadn't left. I knew who she was because I had seen her before in her yard. She was likely having grandmotherly thoughts, "Dumbassed boys, always doin' something stupid."

"Awright, I'll call it for ya," she finally said as she walked back toward the house.

"What the hell you doin' up there in that old tree anyway?"

She didn't expect an answer. It was almost as if she had to decide whether to help or to just leave me there to teach me a lesson.

"I couldn't get your mother, but I got the guys," Allen announced upon his eventual return.

"You got the guys? What the fuck are they going to do?"

"Well, I figured we could carry you out."

Obviously, I wasn't the stupidest kid on the block. Lucky for me, the sound of the ambulance siren had begun to penetrate the underbrush. I looked around and saw that Allen had brought his brother Randy, our buddy Carlos, and a black kid on crutches. I had seen the crutch boy around, but I didn't know him. He was with Carlos, and he appeared to have a broken leg. He was in a femur cast, and it was visible because he was wearing dungarees with one leg slit all the way up the side. He didn't say anything. He just kept looking down at me and then up to where the branch used to be. Then he shook his head, spit in the dirt, and turned away.

The medics, a man and a woman, stabilized my arm and got me on my feet. They were able to walk me out to the ambulance. It was a red station wagon, with a red rotating gumball light on top encased in a glass dome. Nothing like the big boxy ambulances we have today. This was essentially an extra-long car. The woman sat in the back with me and the man was the driver. He slammed the big back door shut before going around to the driver seat. We were perched on a bench that ran from front to back on one side of the ambulance. There were no safety belts. An empty stretcher sat on the other side. In the movies, that stretcher always rolled out the door. It occurred to me that it couldn't happen in real life because it was clamped tightly to the wall. I thought it would have been cool to get carried out on that bad boy. The lady was sitting between me and the back door, but her eyes were on the driver as he pulled himself in behind the wheel, and twisted the vehicle away from the curb. My eyes were on Carlos, and the black kid who had gathered his crutches up into the fold of his right arm as the two of them leaped onto the back step of the station wagon ambulance when it started taking on speed. The female medic's gaze met my eyes and she followed my stare to the back of the station wagon. Her hair-raising scream caused the driver to slam on the brakes. I tumbled to the floor, but the pain I suffered was well worth the laughter. She was still screaming as Carlos assisted our new crutched buddy to hobble away in hysteria.

That's just some of the things boys do. Crutch boy's name was Robazz. He became my closest friend. Now he is doing fifty years to life.

When examining the psychological, sociological, and stereotypical factors leading to delinquency, one should never underestimate the 'fun' factor. Boys and men need to get 'jazzed up.' The trick is to channel the flow of the adrenaline juice toward socially and morally acceptable high jinks. Later in life, I joined the fire department as a volunteer and took up extreme skiing. In time, the fire truck was replaced by a police car. The quest for adventure went on.

1957

I would always long to be a part of the big family
that my father always tried to forget.

They said it was a frigid March morning when they brought me home from the hospital. There was ice on the sidewalks, left from the storm on the night I was born. Mimi, my mom, was always a tiny little thing, never more than ninety pounds. I'm guessing the old man helped her to the door while I rested on the floor of the Ford. They always drove Fords. Semmes would go back and retrieve me while Mom waited in the lobby. He had two babies now. He liked it that way. It made him feel important when people depended on him. My dad, Raphael Semmes Lowry, was the eighth of nine children born to an Irish Catholic family in depression-era Massachusetts. Natick was a warm little town right out of a Thomas Kincaid picture postcard. But the Lowry household was cold. That kind of cold can chill a body for life. That was Semmes.

Grandpa Rudd was on the road most of the time, and Grandma Judith was working on reviving her acting career. The older siblings took care of Semmes. I suspect it was more of a chore than a delight. My little boy father must have felt the wrath of their discontent. He never said much about it. He never said too much about anything unless he was breaking balls or giving advice.

Most of the boys in his family went by their middle names and 'Semmes' was no exception. They were a hard-fighting, heavy-drinking clan, and young Semmes spent most of his childhood being roughed up by his five older brothers while struggling in vain for their approval. At seventeen, he followed them into the Marine Corps. After three years in Korea, he was discharged to New York City where he estranged himself and never looked back. I would always long to be a part of the big family that my father always tried to forget.

Mimi, short for Muriel, was the only child of Colin and Muriel Corbin. Colin emigrated from Barbados as a fourth-grader and immediately set about losing his accent to avoid the torment that grade school boys are so quick to dish out. Nana Muriel was a second- or third-generation mixed breed Irish and German descendant. They were both dead before I was six. Mom didn't take it well. She wasn't cut out for real life. Mimi lived in the fantasy world of novels and old English history. Her petit size and girlish sweetness made men want to nurture and take care of her, from her father to my father and others along the way. She quite nicely filled Semmes' need to be needed. They worked well together, living a solitary yet happy life of interdependence with their only child in a single room in New York City. Semmes sold encyclopedias and drove a taxi. Mimi stayed home and played with her baby toy Kevin.

When the post office hired Semmes around 1959, they were able to rent a sixth-floor apartment with one bedroom in Flushing. I got the bedroom and they slept on the couch. There were advantages to being an only child, but I would have slept in the elevator if I could have had a sibling or two. Still, it was a pretty happy life for me. Unfortunately, my mother was seriously damaged by the death of her own mother two years after Colin. She started getting nervous about going out alone. I didn't notice it.

After eight years, the apartment began getting small. If they wanted a bigger place, they would have to relocate to the other side of town where the rent was lower. It was a trade-off that would lead to the events that shaped my life. It didn't seem so bad at the time. I was in third grade, it was February again and the day after we moved, a crippling snowstorm brought New York City to a halt. School was canceled, and outside my first-floor bedroom window I saw another kid building a snowman. Mimi said I could go out as long as I stayed under the window. His name was Jose. He came from Cuba with his mother and his sister Rosa. Jose senior had been in Batista's army and he was killed by Castro's revolutionaries. He had gotten his family to the sanctuary of the United States hoping that they would return to Cuba once the insurgents were crushed. Things turned out very differently. Jose's mother remarried Alberto, the cigar-chomping superintendent of the building across the street who himself had escaped the communist island about the same time. My new friend and I had no way of knowing where our lives were headed. Jose would be recruited into a gang called Homicide, from Brooklyn. There, he would make his bones in the violence of the Coney Island turf wars. For now, we were just a couple of carefree boys frolicking in the snow and enjoying our fledgling friendship.

As the snow melted, the underbelly of the neighborhood began to expose itself. The windows were opened and the noise of the street began spilling in. It would be several years before things really went down the toilet, but the area was rapidly deteriorating. Jose and I were oblivious. We got to know a lot of other kids, but most of them didn't stay around long. It seemed like everyone was moving out; Randy and Allen, Robert Rizzo, Rusty Akin, and the Coffee boys. They called it 'white flight.' Everybody beat feet. Everybody except little Carlos. Little Carlos moved into a studio apartment in Jose's building with his grandmother. I don't remember what happened to his parents, I'm not certain that I ever knew, but I do remember making fun of Abuela's accent. She wanted a better life for her grandson, but even then, I understood that it was not to be. Carlos was different. He was a short, thin

Columbian guy, and he was very angry most of the time. He was probably compensating for his undersized body and the lack of care that only a mother can give. No opponent was too big or too tough for Carlos. It was a Napoleon thing. He took some butt whippings, but he had heart. The heart was a valuable commodity for the survival of a street hood.

One particularly clammy morning in mid-July, there was a shriek and a loud dull thud at the back of my building. I was jolted from my sleep. My father burst into my room as I was tugging down on the rope that lifted my Venetian blinds. There, on the pavement, lay a young woman. She was face down on the ground and her hair was beginning to soak up the blood running from the front of her head. The roof loomed six stories above her and the leap should have killed her on impact, but it didn't. A faint murmur could be heard from the side of her face. As if, by some instinct, Semmes whirled around and snatched my mother from the room before she could see. He sheltered her from everything, but the world was beginning to penetrate his fortress and he was helpless in holding it back. She wasn't taking it well. Little Mimi was becoming more reluctant to venture out alone. She slept until noon every day and had begun to develop a minor tremor. It must have been the commotion that woke her. This would be way more than she could handle.

"Call the police and keep your mother away from that window," the old man barked.

Then he grabbed a sheet and bolted out the door. After I made the call, I left my mother sobbing in the kitchen and returned to the window. Semmes draped the sheet over the rumpled young woman and sat next to her holding her hand. He spoke softly to this dying stranger while his khaki-colored slacks slowly turned red. That was Semmes. He was always my hero, even after the drinking began.

The woman landed on the sidewalk on the left. My bedroom window was on the first floor to the right of the chimney. The living room window was to the right of that. The cozy little benches weren't there back then.

GO ALONG OR GO UNDER

The street is a seductress; cunning and deceitful, fascinating, stunning, exciting, and alluring. If there comes a time in a boy's life when he must choose which side of the street to walk on, the wrong choice may destroy him.

The neighborhood was already 'changing' when I moved in. I didn't recognize it because my family was part of the change. People were seeking affordable housing for growing families. For some of us, it was a chance to gain a little elbow room. For others, it meant a move-out. Those who had lived there long enough saw the shift, and they didn't like it. The deli gave way to a bodega, the bank became a Baptist church, and people started locking their doors.

My parents' bedroom looked out from the ground floor onto a busy Sanford Avenue. Cars and trucks went up and down all night long. In the summer, the windows were open because we didn't have air conditioning. Apparently, the utility fees were included in the rent. If the superintendent saw an air conditioner in your window, your rent would go up to five dollars a month. And the increase wasn't just during the hotter months. It was five dollars more for twelve months per year. That was huge! At least it was more than my old man could handle or more than he was willing to shell out. He would rather sweat his balls off in the middle of a sweltering New York City August night, than pay a fee he felt was unjust. Semmes was a stubborn Irishman who stood on principals. I remember going to the movies with him and my mother. They had a smoking section in the 1960s and he was enjoying a cigar. The theater was playing a double feature. That's when you got to see two new movies for the price of admission. It was fairly common back then and a relatively inexpensive way for families to spend an afternoon. They used to play cartoons between the shows as well as newsreels, short films, and coming attractions. Sometimes, a guy named Will Rogers would come on and make an appeal for his charity. Then the ushers would pass around tin cans with little slits at the top like the collection plate in church. You could throw in some change or not. No pressure. What they did not show between the features were advertisements. Now, of course, it's quite common. But not then. Not except for this particular afternoon when the projector sprayed an Oldsmobile advertisement onto the big screen. I have to tell you, my father lost it. He put down the cigar and started a rhythmic clap while yelling, "Boo commercials. Nooo commercials. Boo commercials." The ushers came running over and told him that he had to stop. He replied that he would stop when they turned off the commercials. He paid a fee to see those movies and he didn't believe he should be subjected to sponsorships. "Boo commercials. Nooo commercials."

They threw him out. Not bodily of course, he would have hung them from the sconces on the wall. But they put on the lights, shut off the projector, and told him that he had to get out. My mother was mortified, but I thought it was pretty cool. And I believed he was right.

So, there we were on this muggy summer night, with the windows open, no breeze, and a constant barrage of heavy metal traffic sounds intruding on our privacy. Suddenly, the road noise was pierced by the screams of a woman and some guy yelling back at her. I heard it too in the back of the apartment, and I hurried to my parents' window to see some big pimpy-looking dude tuning up this working girl outside on the sidewalk, right in front of our place. Right away, Semmes Lowry, USMC, was on his way out the door to rescue the damsel. This time, however, my mother's timid common logic prevailed. She demanded that he not intrude and they called the police instead. This was before the 911 emergency number went online. Back then, a person had to dial the operator and ask to be connected to the police, or dial the station house direct. It didn't take long for the cops to arrive. The woman was lying on the trunk of a car and the guy was busy smacking her around real good and yelling something about how it better not happen again, when she spotted the squad car sliding slowly up to the scene. Just then, to my young naïve surprise, she vaulted off of the car and draped herself over the pimp's shoulders. The patrolmen didn't even get out of the cruiser. The passenger cop was making some inquiries as the couple quickly adopted an "everything's cool here officer" kind of posture. Well, the man did anyway. She was holding on like a fighter getting ready to go down for the count, praying for the bell. Mimi and Semmes were flabbergasted that the police weren't doing anything. How could they not even get out of the car? Were they afraid? I, on the other hand, read the scene right away. This was our first time witnessing an event like this in our changing neighborhood. Obviously, the cops had seen it many times before. No point in rushing into a domestic squabble only to wind up getting attacked by the "victim." These two had obviously reconciled. The woman realized the error of her ways and they would live happily ever after. Mission accomplished. Back in service. That event repeated on me like a sour belch when I was on patrol duty years later. Every time I had to respond to a domestic squabble, I always took a step back and hoped that things would calm themselves down before we, the common enemy, arrived. Most of the time, that worked.

That was the kind of drama playing out in my world when I was a kid. I stepped out of my apartment into the hallway, on my way to school one morning, only to find a heroin junkie nodding out on the steps leading to the floors above. His mouth was hanging open, eyes rolled back into the lid shades, drool dripping on soiled sneakers with no laces, and a Newport cigarette literally burning through his fingers. He didn't feel it. I had no idea what was wrong with the guy until I mentioned it to one of the new kids on the block.

"He a dope fiend man! What, you ain't never seen a dope fiend before?"

The neighborhood wasn't the only thing changing. What was also changing was my ability to take care of myself. I was closing in on my thirteenth birthday when I started getting my ass kicked on a fairly regular basis. If I fought one guy, one of his friends would jump in. I was a skinny, little white boy and I was losing the ability to hold my own. There was this one particular kid called Tookie. They said his father nicknamed him that because he used to take things. That could have been true, but his old man was long gone so there was no way to verify. One particular day, Tookie was walking with Carlos and two other kids. I was surprised to see Carlos hanging with them. Tookie always had some shit to say to me and this day was no different.

"Yo man. What-choo looking at? Yeah, that's right. They with me," he gestured toward the other boys, "And if you mess with one, two, or three, you gonna hafta mess with me."

Then he told me that I had to cross the street any time I saw him coming down the sidewalk. After that, I hid from him the first couple of times when he came down the block, but I quickly realized that I could not live like that in my own town. So, the next time he came my way, I refused to cross, and I didn't hide. In fact, I made sure he saw me standing there.

"Yo muthah fuckah, why the fuck you ain't take yo crackah ass across that street?"

"Because I don't feel like it," I said.

I was scared, but he was alone with no one to impress. This was my lucky day. What happened next would dramatically alter the course of my life.

"We gonna hafta fight now white boy."

"Whatever you say."

I thought about ending that sentence with a "muthah fuckah" of my own, but I stopped short.

Tookie was only slightly taller than I, and just about the same age. He looked at me, right in my face, for a good long time. He wore big, thick square glasses on plain black frames with a tattered and knotted athletic strap around the back of his head. They looked like the bottoms of a couple of Coke bottles. They didn't soften him any. Those eyeglasses staring at me made me feel like he was looking right into my heart to see if I was bluffing.

"I'm gonna letchoo slide this time man, but I may hafta wup yo ass another time. Whatchoo doin later?"

"Why?"

"Maybe you wanna come down by the B wing and see what's up. We probably gonna go do something."

"I don't know," I replied.

I was starting to feel pretty good about this. I just got an invitation to hang out with the new kids. The tough kids. The kids nobody fucked with. The "colored" kids.

"What time you gonna be there?"

"I don't know man! Later! Why you ask so many God damn questions? Yaw punk-ass probably ain't even allowed to stay out after dark. Mamma says you gotta be home."

That was the challenge I knew I had to accept. My instincts told me if I didn't show up at Tookie's building that night, I would never get another chance. And I would be crossing the street every day, or taking the beating for not doing it.

"I'll be there. Just don't leave me hangin alone."

"Oh, you givin me orders now. Aw right. We'll see. We'll just see if you show up."

I made my debut at the B wing that night in response to Tookie's kind invitation and met some of the boys that I had seen around.

"Oh, so you really showed?" Tookie asked, "What the fuck you doin here? Whatdidchoo think I was serious?"

I was bewildered and a little bit more than nervous.

"I'm just fuckin whitchoo man. Hey y'all, this here's the white boy I was tellin y'all about."

He put his hand on my shoulder. "He almost got an ass-kickin' today, but I let him slide. Now he thinks he wanna hang out."

The crew sized me up, asked me some questions, and goofed on my clothes a little bit, but they let me hang. And I went back the next day.

That's my parents' bedroom window, and the bathroom window just to the left.

The B wing alley hasn't changed much except there were no trees back in the day.
The wall down at the end is where we drew our stickball box.

JANE PARKER

It didn't feel like stealing, it was just another adventure.

My new friends played a lot of games. One of the games was dodgeball. In dodgeball, two teams line up opposite each other with a demarcation line in between. Somebody sets up the boundaries.

"The line is at that window. Our team can back up to the wall and y'all can go back as far as the fire escape ladder."

We played murder ball like we played everything else, in the alleyway alongside the "B wing" of the Regency House. That was the building next to mine. It had an "A wing" and a "B wing." No basement. The B wing was where the action always took place. The apartment building itself sat on the west side of the alley. The east side of the alley was bordered by a basic four-foot chain link fence. It was the kind of fence with the crimped top so you could climb or hop it easily, without fear of tearing apart your pants or your arm or your nutsack. On the other side of the fence was a dirt runway about four feet wide and overgrown with weeds. It ran from Sanford Avenue to 41st Road, and next to it there was the wall of the garage of my building. This divided buildings one and two from building three in my complex.

So, there was the B wing, the alley, the fence, the dirt runway, and my garage all running parallel to one another. I could take my elevator one story down to the basement, walk through the catacomb, pass the clubhouse, come out the back door, and climb the stairs to the garage roof. From there I would observe the goings-on at the B wing ally. It was also a great spot for an ambush in a game of 'army' or something more serious. If there was something happening at the B wing, I could swing myself over the side of the roof, hang down, and drop the other six feet or so to the soft dirt below. Then I'd hop the fence and get into it.

Once the boundaries were set for dodgeball, we would designate captains and choose our sides. In order to see who got the ball first, the captains would "choose it out." That usually meant "odds or evens." That was the simplest and fastest way to get it done. One captain would call odds, the other evens. Somebody would say "One twice three, shoot." Each captain would throw one finger or two. If the sum of the fingers was odd, the odd man would get a point and vice-versa for evens. Best two out of three wins. It usually worked well unless there was a dispute over a 'late finger.' These disputes could be resolved with a do-over, a fistfight, or a full team brawl which often ended the game before it started. Anyway, the winner's team got the ball first.

The secondary object of the game was to throw the ball and hit someone on the other team. If you hit a guy from the other team, he was out. If the other guy caught the ball on the fly, the thrower was out. The team with the last man standing would win. The real object of the game was to hit somebody in the face. If you could clock somebody solid in the face, it didn't matter who won or lost, everybody would just remember how bad one of the guys got smashed in the face. And the smashee was destined to have his balls busted for the foreseeable future unless he kicked the smasher's ass. The problem with the 'real object,' to hit somebody in the face, was that the distance between the players was usually sufficient to preclude any real pain or blood-producing injury. Hence the advent of murderball. Murderball was a free for all version of dodge ball. The players were trapped between the building and the fence, but tighter outer boundaries would be established so that we could play in a much smaller rectangle or square. This was the ball version of cage fighting. There was no center line, no teams, and basically no rules. It was every man for himself. The game started with a jump ball and proceeded from there. You could get close enough to another player to splatter his nose or give him a hell of a shiner. That kind of game could build you some street cred. If you fled the boundaries you were a punk. Then you would have to stand in front of the wall and let everybody take a shot at your face from a distance of about ten feet, like a firing squad only one at a time.

I was hanging with these guys now. These were some raw dudes, and they played some cool games. All the other neighborhood kids I knew were intimidated by them, but now I was beginning to feel as though I was part of their group. I was fitting in, and I liked it.

Jose was a regular part of the crew now and so was little Carlos. Robazz and Kasseem were brothers. Kasseem was older and he had an ice-cold mean streak. I once saw him burn a mouse to death because she ate one of her babies. He was a hustler, a schemer, and a smooth con man. He was both ruthless and charismatic. He could have been a successful business tycoon, attorney, or military leader. If Kasseem couldn't seduce you or con you, he'd terrorize you into submission. One thing made him especially frightening. He had this vein that ran vertically through his forehead. If that vein was popping out, you better get out of his way. Robazz was tough but more compassionate. Sometimes, you could catch a glimpse of his softer side. He was the kind of guy who preferred to talk things over until he could persuade the other guy. But it was a grave error to mistake his empathy for weakness. I watched him open up some guy's chest with a switchblade one night. In fairness, it was self-defense. Then there was Thumper and Ballah. They were Tookie's half-brothers from another father. Ballah was about 10 years old at that time. A fierce fighter and an accomplished thief, he could hang with the big boys. He was always in the company of Thumper who himself was quite a thief and very protective of his little brother. Thumper was about 13. They were both small in comparison to others their age and very skinny. I recall them also being sick much of the time. It seems like their noses were always running. But they had a knack for sniffing out money. They often traveled with a nasty little Jack Russell mixed breed mutt named Champ. Champ's food was at times sprinkled with gun powder which surely took its toll on his tiny brain. Nobody messed with Champ. They were two crazy fucking kids with a sick fucking dog.

Anyway, Thumper was a great thief with a talent for escape. We slipped into the YMCA around 2 am one blustery autumn night to swim in the pool. It went well until we started jumping off the high diving board. That attracted the attention of the night manager and the chase was on. We all scooped up our clothes and made a dash for the exits. I got caught in a dead-end with Thumper. There was an industrial style rolling laundry cart there in the hallway. Just as the guy burst through the door, Thumper flipped the laundry basket over on himself and disappeared. Why didn't I think of that? The guy didn't know how many people he was chasing and I certainly wasn't going to tell him, or the nice police officer who gave me a lift to the 109 Precinct, that Thumper was hiding under there.

Thumper was also a true sociopath. When we were younger, it wasn't as much of an issue because he was always a lightweight, but as we grew older, he became more dangerous. There are rumors that several years after I left the gang, he made his brother shoot one of our friends named LeyLey. That left LeyLey in a wheelchair for life. Thumper wanted Ballah to shoot Robazz too. Allegedly, Ballah fired several shots at him, but Robazz was able to literally dodge the bullets.

"Yo Kev, where you goin man?" Thumper enquired.

It was probably around 6:30 in the evening. We had been playing murderball, dodgeball, and stickball all day. Now it was time for me to go home for dinner. By now, Semmes would have a load on. No matter how stewed he got, he always made dinner. If I didn't get home to eat, that would be my ass.

"I gotta go. I'll be back after I eat."

"You better get your crackah butt back here later. We goin to get some cookies tonight."

'*Cookies*?' I thought. '*I wonder who's going to give us cookies.*'

The old man was still a pretty mellow drinker back then. Mom and he used to bicker, but the violence didn't start until after his 'indiscretion.'

"Where have you been all day?" Mom asked.

"Out."

"What have you been doing?" she persisted.

Why do mothers do that? They know they're not going to get any genuine information from their teenage boys, yet they never give up trying.

"Nothin."

"Who were you with?"

"Just some friends."

"What the hellsamatter with you? You forgot how to talk? Owwt. Nuuthinn. Free-ends."

My father communicated through mockery. That was just his thing. He did it to everybody, not just me. Everybody loved or pitied my mother. But my father just pissed most people off.

"What's for dinner, Dad?" A change of subject would usually do the trick if he was buzzed enough to miss his train of thought.

"Tuna burgers."

That was Star-Kist Tuna-burgers. A Lowry Friday night favorite.

"Cool Dude."

"Yeah right. Cool-dude boy," he burped.

It worked. The limited chatter that followed surrounded his back injury and how it might someday be his ticket out of the post office. Nothing else was said about my communication skills. When supper ended, I bolted.

"Where are you going now?" Mom asked.

"Out."

She didn't push it this time. "Be home by ten."

Not a chance.

'Hadda save some room for those cookies,' I thought as I cruised past the laundry room, through the basement tunnel, out the back, and up the garage roof steps. I scanned the B wing, but I didn't see anyone I knew. There were a couple of girls sitting on the bench. They looked to be about twelve.

"Excuse me. You girls know Robazz?"

"If we did, we wouldn't tell you."

Okay, that was helpful. I leaned back against the bricks and gazed around the roof. My pupils strolled from window to window. Many apartments looked right out onto the garage roof. I thought that I wouldn't like living in one of those apartments where someone could walk up those stairs and peer right in. Then I thought it might be fun to go peer in somebody's window. Maybe I could catch a lady coming out of the shower. No, that wouldn't be right. It could be somebody's mom. What if it was my mom? I wouldn't like that. I might have to kick somebody's ass. As long as his ass wasn't too big. Semmes would damn sure kick his ass no matter how big he was.

Presently, my eyes came to rest on a six-pack of Coke on a windowsill just inside an open window.

Man, if I grabbed that and brought it over to the B wing, I'd be some kind of big shot. Too bad I don't steal.

"Yo, white boy! Whatchoo doin up there muthah fuckah? We gonna go get some cookies or what?" It was Kasseem barking.

"Yeah man," I leaped from the roof, "Who's got them?"

"We gotta go get em."

He had the whole crew in tow already, his brother Robazz, Carlos, the psycho brothers Thumper and Ballah, and Jose.

"How you doin man?" asked Robazz. "You up for this?"

"Definitely! I love cookies."

"I mean, are you ready to take 'em?"

"Take 'em how?"

"You'll see," he laughed.

We walked down Sanford Avenue and turned left on Lawrence Street in the direction of the Flushing Meadow Park, the scene of the 1963 World's Fair. Several of the original structures still existed. The giant globe or 'Unisphere,' as we called it, is probably the most photographed to this day. The most famous, however, are the towers that turned into space ships at the end of *Men in Black*.

Several blocks passed underfoot as we bantered.

"What the fuck kinda sneakers you got man?" Thumper quizzed.

"PF Flyers. Why?"

"Man, check out this guy's skips" Thumper demanded to uproarious laughter.

"You need some Cons man."

He hoisted his cuffed Wrangler jeans to expose the trademark star of the side of his Converse high top.

"Don't get the ones that slip and slide, go get the ones with the star on the side." He sang the jingle and did a little Bo Jangles dance in the street holding up both pant legs as if he were bouncing through a puddle trying to keep his jeans dry. More laughter and unanimous agreement.

"Yeah and what's up with them pants man. Looks like the skips were smoking reefer and your pants got high."

This sent everyone into a frenzy of hilarity. The bottoms of my dungarees were ankle-length. They were 'high waters.'

Robazz put an arm around my neck and through tears of amusement he said, "We gotta hook you up man. If you gonna role with us, you gotta know how to dress."

That was my first lesson in street fashion. There would be more. Clearly if I was to earn any respect, I had a lot to learn. No more two-dollar dungarees from Gertz. Only Wranglers were acceptable. In the sneaker department, there were two options: HighTop Converse and Pro-Keds.

After about fifteen minutes, we found ourselves strolling past the guard booth at the gate of 'Jane Parker,' a massive bake factory the size of about three home depot stores. 'Jane Parker' was a subsidiary of A&P Supermarkets. The Great Atlantic and Pacific Tea Company. It was their store label for all their baked goods. This was apparently a major distribution center for the New York City area.

"Whadda we get some kind of discount here?" My ridiculously naïve question caused the boys to double over.

"Yeah, a hundred percent," someone replied.

"His punk ass ain't ready for this shit," sneered Ballah. I really wasn't ready. It was clear now that the cookies were going to come from the loading dock of that factory. I'm Catholic. I can't steal.

"Anybody comes outta there without a box gets their hangout card revoked," boomed Kasseem. "And if ya get popped, no names." An obvious reference to the street code of silence. If you get caught, you don't rat anybody else out.

The facility looked like Stalag 13. It was surrounded by an eight-foot chain link fence with a crimped top. The loading dock was about fifty yards from the fence and well lit. Some employee parking would provide cover. We could see boxes stacked everywhere. There was some activity, but it was confined to only a few tractor-trailers being loaded. Adrenaline was beginning to gush. If I didn't do this, I would be out of the group and back to getting my ass kicked daily. But strangely, it didn't feel like stealing, it was just another adventure. These guys really knew how to have fun.

Robazz grabbed my arm. "Stick with me Kev. I'll show you how it's done. We goin' for the coffee cakes."

At the darkest part of the yard, down by the Van Wycke Expressway overpass, there were some cinderblocks loose at the base of the fence.

"This is where the boxes come out," my mentor explained.

Ballah was able to slip under the fence through the hole in the blocks. The rest of us scaled the metal and dropped inside. We crouched in the darkness until everyone was in.

"Let's do this," someone exclaimed in a stage whisper.

I swore I could hear my heart beating as we bolted for the cover of the parked cars. Robazz and I stole along the line of bumpers and tail lights to the right flank of the others, putting some distance between us and the bakery workers loading the trucks. Ahead, toward the end of the loading platform, were a couple more men apparently on a smoke break. I just knew they would see us.

The loading dock was two trailer-lengths away, across a vast and dimly illuminated asphalt desert.

"They're gonna see us, man!" I whispered.

"Just get low, move fast, and stay with me," Robazz answered. "We gotta make it between those two trucks. I'll jump up and toss you two cases. When we get clear, we run back to the cars. Okay?"

"Okay."

I had never experienced such an exhilarating combination of terror and excitement. I actually caught myself pretending we were Special Forces combat marauders pillaging some Vietnamese supply depot. Charlie was everywhere, but they never expected us to be there.

One of the smokers must have cracked a joke which got them all laughing and giving each other five. That was our cue. We broke across the lot and dove for the cover of the eighteen-wheelers. A quick peek at the smokers and we realized that we had arrived undetected. Robazz scanned our target zone with the composure of a Navy Seal. Then, he slithered up the four-foot wall and over a well-worn red rubber bumper. I guessed that the bumper kept the trailers from crushing the concrete wall. He dragged himself along the floor to the base of a wooden pallet stacked with our booty; shipping cartons loaded with 1 or 2 dozen individual boxes of goodies.

"It ain't coffee cake," he breathed.

"What is it?" I demanded softly.

"Oatmeal cookies."

Now, in a catcher's crouch, he glanced left to right as if looking for something else. He looked back at me and said, "I hate oatmeal cookies."

"Fuck it! Just get 'em!"

Robazz tossed me one box before we heard the voices. It was the Viet Cong. The smokers were coming. I made a frantic pulling motion with both hands open, palms facing my chest to urge him toward me. He grabbed another crate, leaped from the loading dock, and rolled under the truck where I was already hiding. With our backs to the cinderblocks, we sat upright as the floor of the trailer above began to groan with the clomp of work boots and metal wheels. They were loading the truck. It sounded like they were using one of those manual forklifts. Because I was so riveted by the activity above, I never heard the sound of tearing cardboard at my left side. The position of the trailers tightly lined alongside each other precluded the entry of all but a little light. It was enough for me to turn to see Robazz biting off a chunk of an oatmeal cookie sandwich.

"What the fuck are you doing?" I whispered.

"I'm hungry," he mumbled through a mouthful.

"But you HATE oatmeal cookies!"

We had to cover our mouths to muffle our laughter. I thought Robazz was going to choke on the crumbs.

When the truck's engine began to rumble, we snapped back to reality. Someone dragged the rolling door down the back of the trailer and the latch clanged shut. Two sharp raps of the aluminum were apparently the signal that the load was secure. The lanky truck eased away from the dock as we sat frozen between the big black back tires. Then the truck was gone and we found ourselves totally exposed. A quick look around led to a reckless dash for the parking line. After a survey of the scene, we determined that it was safe to advance to the fence and escape enemy territory clinging to our cookies. Oatmeal never tasted so good.

There would be other forays into 'Jane Parker' that summer, and into supermarkets, and then department stores. The stealing kept getting easier and bigger as the years rolled by.

My garage roof. From there you could get a bird's eye view
of the B-wing on the other side.

PERIPHERAL VISION

In the street, both danger and opportunity present themselves all around you. Survival depends on your ability to develop an eagle x-ray vision.

My all-time favorite cop show was a Steven Bochco series called *Hill Street Blues.* There was a character in that program called 'Mick Belker.' Detective Belker was a grown-up version of 'Pig Pen' from '*Peanuts.*' He was a sentimental character who loved his mother but couldn't get along with average people. He used to bite the prisoners' legs like a rabid K9, a little Bochco poetic license. What made Belker so special though was that he was street savvy. He saw things that few people, including other cops, could see. Mick had an eagle x-ray vision. He had a 360-degree view of his post and his eyes penetrated through the superficially obvious, extracting the reality of events lurking below the surface. "Read the street hair bag." That was his slogan. Whichever side you're on, you have to be able to read the street.

Kids tend to spend enormous amounts of time engaged in unproductive behavior, taking all sorts of risks in an unending pursuit of something to do. Some guys never grow out of that. At thirteen years old, I was just getting started. We would often spend afternoons hanging around Woolworths. Older folks called it the "5 and 10." Even older people called it the "5 and Dime." Woolworths was such a popular store that they had an exit directly into the subway station at Roosevelt Avenue and Main Street. One afternoon, a couple of the brothers decided to snatch some fish from the basement level of the store. I'm not talking about flounder; I'm talking about live fish for a home aquarium. They were guppies or mollies or some other little crappy 'tropical' fish. Who steals guppies? None of us even had a tank to put them in. Somebody may have had a buyer lined up, I don't know for sure. The fish apparently came into the store in a big plastic bag. Some employee put the whole bag into a large tank full of water and left it there so the creatures could acclimate to the water temperature in the store. One of the guys, I think it was Thumper, pilfered a brown paper bag from behind one of the counters. All the stores used brown paper bags for the customers' purchases. It didn't matter if you were buying light bulbs from a hardware store or bread from Trade Rite, you would be taking it home in a brown paper bag. Then those same brown paper bags would be reused for school lunches, overnight bags, and trashcan liners. It was always a race to get the soggy sack of garbage to the incinerator chute before it broke open all over the hallway floor.

Anyway, they got a hold of one of those bags and they headed over to the tank with the prize fish in it. My job was to lookout. Security always watched the black kids. The mere presence of a couple of "colored" boys, in any department store, would provide an instant diversion for me. We would always go in separately and I could move about relatively unnoticed while the others were watched closely. I could do most of the stealing with impunity while my boys wandered around like pied pipers with the house dicks in tow. On that particular day, however, the heat appeared to be off. We seemed to be operating undetected. With our normal roles abandoned, the other guys snatched the fish and tucked them into the brown paper bag. They sauntered by me, and I took the handoff.

I meandered toward the steps leading up to the subway exit, pretending to glance at the items on the shelves while scouring the zone for store detectives. Feeling pretty confident, I climbed the stairs and slid through the glass doors to the token platform. I was out. I was safe. No big deal. We had pulled off little shoplifting trips like that dozens of times. Turning to look back through the window, I saw that the guys were still moving about the basement looking for another score. '*They're getting cocky,*' I thought to myself, so I hung around out there. Not a good move. I was pacing back and forth with the heisted little swimmers in the brown paper sack, occasionally taking a look through the window. '*Those assholes are gonna get popped,*' I said to myself. Suddenly I felt a tap on my shoulder. I looked over to see a store manager had come out the door. He had seen me out there acting furtively and I drew his curiosity. He read the street.

"Whadda you doin out here kid?" he demanded.

"Nuthin."

"Who you waitin for?" he persisted.

"Nobody."

"What's in the bag?"

This guy knew he was on to something and I had to admire him at the moment. He was street savvy like Mick Belker. He was a nerdy-looking store manager with a name tag and a short tie. It dangled about six inches above his belt buckle and kind of draped over his belly to around where his naval probably was. But this guy saw through the situation and recognized something lurking below the surface in the subway station. I had forgotten all about that guy until a chilly autumn night in the early 80s when my partner came over the air requesting assistance.

"421 to headquarters, request assistance at the diner at Long Beach and Mott. Possible stolen car occupied in the parking lot."

I took the call along with two or three other units, but I was several minutes away.

Suddenly, "421, subject jumped the curb. In pursuit east on Mott!"

"416, I got him."

416 was assisting in the pursuit. I hit the siren and stomped on the gas, north on Long Beach Road.

"421, we're northbound Oceanside Road."

They were moving! There's no way I was going to catch up. *If I run parallel, I could cut the prick off if he makes a left and heads west,* I thought to myself.

"420, I'm running parallel, north on Long Beach Road," I blurted into the mike.

416 was able to put out the plate number and a description of the occupants as a male driver and a female passenger. It was a dealer plate and headquarters confirmed a signal 15, stolen vehicle. Somehow Bob Benzenberg in car 421 had recognized the car from a report he had taken at Becker Chevrolet that day or the day before. That was heads up ball.

"407, I'm in front of them North on Oceanside. Advise units I will attempt a slowdown."

407's plan was to let the fleeing Camaro get up close on his tail and then he would hit the brakes. The other units would drop back a bit to avoid a pile up. Good plan, but it didn't work. 407 hit the brakes and the suspect buzzed around him and blew right by, followed by 421 and 416. I was hoping the guy would turn left, westbound on a side street and I could box him in. The side streets were narrow and my old Dodge Diplomat was wide enough to close off his escape route.

"421, he turned right, eastbound on Foxhurst."

That was it; I was out of the game. I hung around up north for a while in case he doubled back, but it never happened. When they got to Sunrise Highway, the guy made another right and headed for the Meadowbrook Parkway. They had to be flying! It was like a high-speed conga line. When the pursuit reached the Meadowbrook, the Communications Bureau supervisor shut it down, and I headed back toward the diner. The boys wouldn't give up just because the boss called off the pursuit, but they would surely slow it down. It was a valiant effort, but that guy was in the wind. I started to wonder why he had been sitting in the diner parking lot. As I approached the establishment, I noticed a couple standing just outside the doors at the top of the steps leading to the entrance. They weren't talking, but they were glancing around. That's when I flashed back to the "5 and 10" and the sack full of guppies.

The guy in the hot Camaro was waiting for that couple to bring the take out. Then they'd all be heading home. I was reading the street and I was going to blow this caper wide open, but I needed a plan and I needed it quick. The couple had come down the steps and was crossing Long Beach Road. Obviously, they hadn't called a taxi so I had a little time.

I swung the Dodge around and tailed the duo at a distance while rehearsing my lines. I would stop them and split them up. The guy would tell me where they were from and that would be about it. The rest would be bull shit. The girl was the weak link. I would tell her that I wasn't interested in locking anyone up, but that the Camaro had slammed into a wall and caught fire. Both people were burned alive. At that point she would break down crying, "Oh my God. That was my sister in that car." It was ice cold, but I wouldn't allow her to grieve for long. Once I got the ID on the perps, I would come clean. They'd hate me. *'Better get back up. I will request assistance before I tell them the truth,'* I surmised.

I slid over to the curb and got out of the car.

"Excuse me. Can I talk to you a minute?" The girl froze and the guy walked right over to me. This was working well.

"What's your name?"

"Anthony."

"Whadda you doing here?"

"We were at the diner and now we're goin home. Why?"

"Where's home," I persisted.

"Brooklyn," snapped Anthony.

'This is it,' I thought. 'I got 'em.'

"Stay here a minute Anthony, I wanna talk to your friend."

Anthony was being very cool. Too cool. An innocent guy would have looked more confused. He would probably want to know more about what was going on and why I stopped them.

"Just sit tight. I'll be with you in a minute."

Walking toward that girl I was actually thinking about the praises I was going to get from the veteran officers and how pissed Benzenberg was going to be. I was about three years out of the police academy, and I was about to pull off one of the greatest pieces of detective work anyone had ever dreamed of. But a strange feeling started creeping up on me as I grew closer. I knew her. But it wasn't like a police officer knows the local shit heads on his post, it was more like Harry Chapin recognizing the architect's wife in the taxi song.

What happened next is one of the most bizarre coincidences I've ever experienced or heard of. I have played this event over in my mind hundreds of times.

"Heidi? Heidi, is that you?"

"I don't know you," she lied.

"The hell you don't." I grabbed her arm. That got Anthony running.

"Yo, what's goin on? You know dis guy?"

"Tell him the truth. You're Heidi Greeble from Canarsie," I said.

Anthony was getting really agitated and this whole thing was going to shit. I had completely lost my focus, but I wasn't about to let this guy jap me.

"I used to go out with him," said Heidi as she started to cry.

It was way more than going out. We were steady for about three solid years and I was actually out with her the night I met my wife. We were skating at the Roller Palace in Sheepshead Bay. Annie just rolled into my life. I loved Heidi, but Annie is my soul mate, and I knew that from the minute we met. After all the time Heidi and I spent together, I took the coward's way out. I should have told her it was over. I should have thanked her for all the good times and apologized for falling for someone else. Instead, I didn't explain anything, I just stopped calling her. She called me every day for a while. She kept leaving me messages and I just kept ignoring them. I never saw her again until that night across the street from the diner. I had guessed that after I scammed her about the fiery tragedy that befell the people in the stolen car, the girl at the diner would hate me. I never guessed that she already did.

"Haven't you screwed me enough in my life? Whadda you gonna do now, arrest us for stealing that car?"

"Shut up, stupid!" Anthony screamed.

"Hey you shut up man," I got right in his face. "This girl just saved your ass from takin a collar." I turned my back.

"No, I'm not goin to arrest you. I'm gonna take you to the train and send you home."

And that's what I did. No one spoke in the car and we didn't say good-bye. I never breathed a word of it to another cop. I never asked Heidi or Anthony about the couple in the Camaro. They just got out of my car and I watched them walk away.

"Whadda you doin out here?" the store manager demanded.

"Nuthin."

"Who you waitin for?" he persisted.

"Nobody."

"What's in the bag?"

"I don't know."

"You don't know? Whadda you mean you don't know?" He was starting to get a little miffed but confused. I had him.

"Some black kid asked me to hold it for him for a minute while he went to get some candy. Now I don't know where he went. The kid told me he'd get me a Mallo Cup."

I made it look like I was looking for the phantom fish thief while the real crooks looked back at me from the up-going escalator.

"Was it those guys?" he asked.

"Naw. This guy was real dark-skinned and he had a pimple on his head."

I was laying it on now.

"Lemme see that bag." He snatched it away.

"Do you know these are stolen fish?"

"Damn, that sneaky bum! How could he do that to me?" I tried to sound white.

I wondered where I was getting this shit from.

"Well that should be a lesson to you son. Never trust anyone. Now get outta here."

"Thanks, Mister. Sorry."

I doubt Mick Belker would have fallen for that.

SKI

Ski was one badass anti-crime cop. He was the first guy who ever put the cuffs on me. Ski seemed like he knew everything that was going on in the 109.

It was chilly that night. I remember because we saw this Spanish dude, wearing a really sharp Eisenhower jacket, walking down Main Street by the bagel store. We were half-joking as we talked about taking him off for his leather just before we got grabbed. We had been milling around Tookie's apartment at the Regency. It was Robazz, Tookie, Bobby Jackson, and me, the macadamia nut in the chocolate bar. Bobby Jackson was Robazz's cousin. They weren't really related, but Bobby had been around as long as the two could remember. Bobby had a very high Afro and a tooth missing in the front of his smile. I doubt that he'd ever been to the dentist or past the fourth grade. Robazz's mom, Marlene, took him in whenever he was homeless. That was often. Tookie's mother, Sylvia, had all four burners cranking on the stove. She wasn't cooking anything. She just liked it hot in the house. It *was* hot in that house. Sylvia had three sons, three daughters, and three bedrooms. It worked.

We didn't have anything to do that particular night. It was the kind of night where boys need to make things happen. We decided to go out for bagels. The bagel store wasn't too far away, down Frame Place, and up the long stretch of 41st Road past Johnnie Tibursky's house and the side of the Prospect movie theater. Frame Place was a side street running off Sanford Avenue in either direction for one block. 41st Road ran parallel to Sanford Avenue from Lawrence Street to Main Street. The bagel store was on the corner of 41st and Main. Instead of going down Frame Place, we cut out through the garage directly onto 41st Road. We always hung onto the garage door as it was going up. You couldn't get more than a finger hold so the competition was to see who could hold on the longest. Bobby won this time. The big wooden door would close automatically after a while, but I pressed the button to close it manually this time. When it was very close to the ground, I rolled under commando style. Across the street, we saw three kids from Corona, high tailing it toward Lawrence Street. You could go down Lawrence Street, cross the street by the Bland House Projects, and walk the bridge along Roosevelt Avenue under the L train past Shea Stadium and into Corona. The L is what we called the elevated number 7 subway tracks.

"I wonder what them niggas doin round here," Robazz recognized them. His grandmother still lived in Corona and he knew a lot of people over there.

"I don't know, but they in some kinda hurry," was my response.

There was a wild party going on at the hippie house. The Grateful Dead was whining inside. A couple of dudes were standing on the steps smoking a joint with some chick in a mini skirt. She looked cold.

"Yo, could I get a hit," Tookie asked.

"Right on, man," the chick said.

She handed him the reefer and went inside.

"Knock yourselves out," belched one of the guys and they both retreated to the party.

"I hate that psychedelic shit," Robazz said, referring to the Grateful Dead music as he took the roach from Tookie.

There wasn't much left, but we smoked it down to a crumb of charred Bambu rolling paper before we moved on.

The next stop was the basketball court at the "site of the Future Boy's Club." Country was out there and we stopped to shoot some hoops.

"Whatchoo doin out here by yawself man?"

"Just fuckin around," Country said.

"We goin ta get some bagels. You wanna come?" I asked. I didn't care much about basketball because I wasn't any good at it.

"Yeah, but I ain't got no cash."

"Then you ain't getting no bagels suckah," Robazz snapped in a mid-layup.

Country got the rebound. "Then I ain't goin. I'm getting cold any damn way." And he took the ball and walked off toward home.

"Country assed Nigga's always looking for a sponsor," Bobby laughed.

Country was new to the neighborhood. He came from South Carolina and he had a backwoods "country" accent so we called him Country. He was about six foot one, with reddish unkempt knapping hair and very bad skin. I guessed he didn't wash his face too often.

We checked the parked cars for unlocked doors as we moved on toward Main Street. You never know what people are going to leave in their glove boxes. Cash, drugs, money, sometimes we got lucky. Not tonight!

When we got up by Jonnie Tibursky's house, we caught him heading in with his friend Doughy. They were both white. Born and raised in Flushing. Tibursky didn't like us and we didn't much like him either, but that didn't stop us from being civil … sometimes.

"Yo, wassup Tibursky," I inquired sarcastically.

"Not much."

"Wassup witchoo Doughy?"

"Nothing. What are you guys doing?"

The rumor was that Doughy only had one lung and that's why he wouldn't fight. His mother died when he was just a kid. Some guys would rank on her if they wanted to stir up some shit. Everybody knew that would piss him off, but he never did anything about it. Sometimes Tibursky would stick up for him. I didn't like it when guys teased him about his mom. Some things were just wrong, but it happened from time to time.

"We just cruising man," I said.

"How Debbie doin?" Tookie had a thing for Tibursky's sister. Tibursky wasn't happy about it and he ignored the question.

"We'll catch you later," he replied and they went on in the house.

We checked the side door of the Prospect movie theater as we cruised by. Sometimes, we would find it open, and we could sneak in to catch the show. If we really wanted to see the movie, we would all chip in and buy one ticket. I would generally be the guy to go in with the ticket. The theater people would always watch the black kids a little harder so I had the best shot at completing the mission. I would loiter around the water fountain near the fire exit for a while until the ushers were out of sight. Then I would pop the door a crack and let the others in. We usually got away with it. Jose and I got caught once when we did it during the day and the light came pouring in. The usher took us to the manager's office. When the guy picked up the phone to call the cops, we burst out the door, through the theater, and out the door by the stage with the popcorn guy in pursuit–all to the excitement of the paying crowd.

The door was locked that night so we continued toward the bagel shop. Most of the boys bought salt bagels. They were about eight cents each. I liked the onion. There was a union guy that used to picket outside the place against non-union labor. He wore one of those wooden signs that had a front, a back, and a couple of shoulder straps holding them together at the top. He wore it like a shirt and it said, "Union Shop." I thought it said, "Onion shop" and I had no idea what the purpose was. The guy would stand there saying, "Pass it by, please. Pass it by, please." He wasn't there that night.

Robazz and I stood outside, munching the warm bread, while Bobby and Tookie got their order. When the Puerto Rican dude passed with the Eisenhower leather, I commented to Robazz. "We should take that muthah fuckah off for that leather, man."

Before Robazz could respond, I found myself slammed against the wall. I had no clue what was going on.

"What the fuck you doin?" Robazz yelled.

Then BAMM! He was right alongside me, bewildered, but still chewing.

"Shut up! You're under arrest."

It was Ski, and three other anti-crime cops cuffing us up. Bobby and Tookie came out with their hands up and they got taken down a little softer.

"What are you locking us up for?" I demanded.

"Mopery," was the response.

As it turned out, the guys we saw running home toward Corona had robbed an elderly couple in the vestibule of an apartment building on Sanford Avenue. Ski and the boys were on the lookout for the perps. The description was two black boys. I don't know how I fit in, but all four of us were on our way to the 109. That was my first time in a police car. They held us and booked us as juveniles. Semmes, Ms. Marlene, and Ms. Sylvia had to pick us up and we all had to go to Family Court. It sounds crazy, but I was excited about being arrested. I got taken down with the crew and I held my own. Against what? I had no clue!

I also have no idea what my charge was, or what the disposition was. They just let Tookie, Robazz, and me go after one court appearance and we didn't have to go back. Ms. Marlene overheard somebody at the court say that they were going to remand Bobby Jackson. He had some priors and no parent came with him to court. She told him to "split" and that's what he did. He took off and didn't look back. We never heard anything else about it. That was our first introduction to Ski. After that, he was watching us all the time.

We were watching him too. The guy was a super cop. He was all over the place. But at six foot five, he really couldn't hide. He had omnipresence. We would hear stories about big arrests he was involved in, and every now and then he would shake us down.

I knew how to play the game. When I had some dirt on somebody outside the click, I would always let Ski know about it. Odds were that I would need somebody to cut me a little slack sometime down the road, and I was taking out a little insurance. But make no mistake, I wasn't his friend and he wasn't mine. If he had a chance to take me down on something big, he never would have thought twice.

It turned out that Robert Kiselewski was a lot more like me than either one of us ever dreamed we'd be. Born the son of Polish immigrants, Kiselewski came up hard. He was the graduate of life in the New York City housing project system. Ski spent his entire career in the 109 and retired as a second grader. That's a second-grade detective. Pretty prestigious. I remember hearing about his promotion from anti-crime to detective. That's how notorious he was on the street.

"Ski got the gold shield," Kasseem said one afternoon after coming home from court. He got busted for something and ran into Ski in the station house.

"That's right, I seen the mother fuckin badge."

Ski was a hard-assed no-nonsense tough fucking cop. He took no shit and would not hesitate to give you a smack. And you know what? We respected him for that. We didn't like him, but we respected him. Street kids live by violence. That's what we understood. Softness and sympathy was a sign of weakness. We weren't looking for friends. The cops had their jobs and we had ours. If the cop was too easy, we would try to take advantage. That's how bad guys are. They might scream, "Police brutality," but only to get over. In the end, it's the tough cops that get results. The others just get pushed around. Ski was a tough cop. Secretly, we all wanted to be like Ski. I wanted to be like Ski. Little did I know, I would be!

Jumping ahead a few decades, some guy got busted in the Sixth Pct. on a burglary rap while I was on duty as the detective supervisor. Joe Skowronski, another tough Polish detective, and a great interrogator had the case. I used to call him Joeski. Skowronski walked into my office shortly after the burglar was brought in.

"What's up Joeski? What ya got goin?"

"Sarge, this guy's looking to make a deal. He said he can give us a murderer in Flushing."

"Well, he's not gonna give *us* a murderer. He might give the *city* a murderer. Did you promise him anything?"

"Nothing."

"See how much you can get from him," I directed, "Then call the 109. But make him go for the burglary first."

Joeski went away. He came back about twenty-five minutes later.

"Okay, boss. The guy gave up the burglary and he gave me the name of the homicide victim in Queens, but nothing else."

"No problem. It's not our case anyway. Call the 109 and see what they want to do."

"I already did," Joeski said. "One of my *paisons* is coming out."

"Whadda you mean?" I asked.

"Another Polack named Kiselewski."

Holy shit! I thought.*Could this be the same guy? Could he still be on the job? How am I going to handle this? This guy knows all about me and I'm not ready for anyone else to know about me. The other cops might not take it right. I might lose their trust.*

"Okay. Good," I said.

Ski showed up wearing a suit. He was just as tall as I remembered. His partner was younger and a little scruffy. By then, I had given the situation a good amount of thought. I decided that Ski probably wouldn't remember me during a brief introduction. So much time had passed and he must have seen a lot of perps along the way. I didn't look or talk anything like I did in those days, and I certainly was in an unlikely position as the deputy commanding officer of a Precinct Squad, a very far cry from where I was the last time we met. And even if he did recognize me, what reason would he have to make trouble for me? I never did anything to him personally and I had turned my life around. I was rehabilitated. *'Fuck it'* I thought.

Still, I chose to keep a low profile during the visit from my old acquaintance on the NYPD. I stayed in my office, and he and his partner weren't there very long.

"Hey, Sarge!"

I looked up from my desk to see Joeski standing in the doorway with Ski hovering behind him.

"This is detective Kiselewski from the 109."

"How are you doing brother?" Ski had walked over to me so I stood up and shook his hand.

"I'm Sergeant Lowry."

"Nice to meet you, Sarge."

"How did it go with our boy? Did he give you anything good?" This was at once surreal, exhilarating, frightening, and reminiscent. There I was, standing in the presence of this cop who I admired, and who had inspired me, and who had arrested me. He was a man who had impacted my life in a highly improbable combination of ways, and yet he was completely oblivious to all of it. To him, I was just another brother in blue. The only thing we shared in his mind was the bond that all police officers share with cops they have never met; unmistakable, but impersonal. He would forget me before his partner started the car outside.

"Nope," Ski replied. "He's fulla shit. Got nothing to offer."

"There will be no deals for him tonight," my resident Pollack chimed in.

"I suppose not," said Ski. "Thanks for trying anyway."

"No problem. Thanks for coming. Sorry, it didn't work out," I said as I shuffled some papers behind my desk.

"Okay, see you next time," Ski offered over his shoulder as he walked away.

THE FAMILY AFFAIR

Perhaps somewhere in another dimension, or some parallel universe, there exists a Kevin Lowry whose life was different. Maybe his parents didn't move to that neighborhood or maybe he found his solace in some socially acceptable manner. I don't know that man. I don't know his wife, his children, or what he does for a living. But I know me and I am most content with the person I have become. I am the sum of my experiences. Although I take no pride in my abhorrent adolescent behavior, I have few regrets. I place no blame, and I seek no justification.

It was 1972 and things were really heating up. Napalmed villages were smoldering in Vietnam, Brooklyn was under siege, and the Bronx was literally burning. Meanwhile, the hottest place in my life could be seen through the peephole of Apartment 1A on Sanford Avenue. Semmes had finally come clean about his dirty little affair with a twenty-something public school teacher named Wendy. Mimi's world was shattered. The story had come to its tragic twist and Camelot was all a lie. What reason was there left for her to live? Violence took hold of our home. Night after night they raged on until dawn. My mother had no life beyond the steel door of our apartment, nothing left inside and no one to turn to. I lost count of her desperate cries for help through half-hearted suicide attempts. She would attack him with kitchen knives and bris-a-brac. The ex-marine warded off the onslaught, slept with one eye open, and periodically destroyed parts of our home in a furious rage. He indulged in work and beer, she in Valium and shock treatments. This was a private war and there was no role for me to play. I escaped to the streets.

A few blocks over, an 18-year-old Puerto Rican named Angel had emigrated from the Bronx. I guess his family was seeking a quieter life. Not Angel. Tucked away in a Goya bean carton with his BVDs was a dungaree jacket, emblazoned with the colors of his "click," 'The Screaming Phantoms.' A bastardization of the French term "clique", click was a 70s street gang. Angel was a recruiter and soon there were a significant handful of Screaming Phantom jackets, parading themselves boldly around the neighborhood. We saw this as a threat.

Kasseem was the alpha in our group. He was about the same age as Angel and he enjoyed the leadership of the younger crew through intimidation, experience, and fear. The emergence of the Phantoms represented a possibility of his loss of dominance. At seventeen, Kasseem had already "done one." He did a bid; a couple of months at the New York City Men's House of Detention. He was tough, but he was also cagey, and he knew he had to play this one right or things could go bad in a lot of different directions.

Kasseem decided to seek counsel from a much older role model named Terry. Terry didn't need a nickname because he was a truly bad motherfucker. He ran a click called 'The Skells,' out of the 'Bland House Projects.' The Bland was on Roosevelt Avenue, just a block off Main Street.

It was a small complex as housing projects go, with only five buildings. But it was a project nonetheless, and it produced its share of extremely dangerous people.

Kasseem set up a meeting with Terry on Terry's terms. He told Kasseem not to show up with the entire crew. That would be disrespectful and might give people the wrong impression over things. Kasseem didn't really understand what wrong impression people might get or even which people Terry was talking about, but he understood the directive. He put together a small 'council.' "I'm takin my bruthah Robazz, Country for some muscle, and the white boy."

Some of the other guys were really pissed about me being chosen to go on such an historic adventure.

"The white boy?" Tookie questioned. "How the fuck he gets to go?"

"Cause he gets ideas, dumbass."

"Muthah fuckah can't fight worth a shit."

"Ain't gonna be no fightin, dumbass."

"Stop callin' me dumb ass God damnit. What kinda ideas you think you gonna need anyway?"

"The kinda ideas that the white boy gets. Awright? ... Awright! Dumbass."

And off we went to meet with 'The Skells,' down at the Bland Houses.

Four of the Skells were black, two were Latinos, and then there was Terry. Terry went about six foot two, with the foundation of a running back. He was a black man, but his hair was straight and pulled into a ponytail about eighteen inches long. I'm guessing that he straightened it. It didn't appear as though it grew that way naturally. They all wore dungaree jackets with the sleeves cut off. The result was more of a dungaree vest. Some had long-sleeved jackets underneath. A few of the vests were emblazoned with the words 'The Skells.' Others just said 'Skells' underlining an image of a grinning human skull sporting a long beard, and a bandanna. These were their 'colors'; their flags of membership in that click. The left front breast on Terry's colors bore the word 'Prez.' It meant President.

Terry was the president of 'The Skells,' and he was holding court by the handball court wall when we arrived. He was clutching a bottle of Boon's Farm Apple wine in his left fist and 'rankin on' some guy's mother while the others laughed obligingly. Or maybe they laughed because it was funny. Either way, if Terry was ranking, you better be laughing. There were no lights on the handball court and it was late, so it was dark. But it never got truly dark in the city as it does in the suburbs. Even on the blackest of nights, the streets produced their own illuminations. It seems to accumulate from store-front signage, apartment house windows, and automobile headlights, and disperse itself all around. So yes, it was dark, but everyone could be seen clearly. A twenty-foot chain link fence separated us from the Long Island railroad pilings that held up the elevated Main Street station. There was a hole in the fence big enough for an adult to pass through, and the dirt on the other side was strewn with every conceivable type of litter. There were the remains of a Schwinn, four or five pocketbooks, somebody's soiled under-pants, a pre-owned feminine napkin, probably pounds of vermin feces, the carcass of a cat, a wooden milk crate, a couple of car tires, and loads of ordinary garbage and paper. The winos had constructed a half-assed roof to drink under on rainy days.

"Yo fellas, here go my boy Kasseem! What it look like Bro-man."

"Hey, wus up Terry?" Kasseem responded. "These are my boys," he gestured towards us.

"This my boy here," he said to the group. "Hey man, I heard you did one!" (meaning a bid in jail), Terry blurted with his arm around Kasseem's neck.

"Yeah man, I did one."

"How'd you do it?" Terry asked.

"Knockin niggahs out!" was the response.

This drew a, "My man," from Terry who held his hand up, chest high, palm facing down. Kasseem thrust his hand out to take the slap. Then Terry turned his hand over and took one from Kasseem. This was the double five slap. There was no such thing as a high five. The high five hadn't been invented back then. The double five slap was the highest form of praise and jubilation and it was offered to Kasseem, in this case, because he did his bid "knockin niggahs out."

"I know why y'all young bloods are here. Them new kids gotcha all shook up, right?"

He didn't really want an answer.

"Y'all came to the right place. We gonna school ya now. Am I right Chico?"

"Joo is right Terry," Chico was Terry's number two. His right-hand man. His main ace duce. Chico was Puerto Rican. He had a tattoo of Jesus on the back of his left hand. If he asked you, "Joo evah meet A-zues (Jesus)?" it meant that you were about to get smacked. That's what I had heard anyway. I never saw it happen, but I have no reason to doubt that more than one person had taken a backhand from Chico and let it slide. 'The Skells' offered collection services to local drug dealers and bookies. They would work for anyone who would pay and collect from anyone who didn't. Chico was the enforcer. He was the disciplinary guy for the gang as well; the "Sergeant-at-Arms." He wore sergeant stripes on the left breast of his jean-vest colors.

Terry took a swig from the apple wine and handed it to Country who did likewise and passed it around. "It's time for y'all to formalize ya shit. Ya gotta git yaw click together. Gitcha selves a name, put it on ya jackets, and stake ya claim. Make sho you fly them colors proud. Then ya elect a prez and lay down some rules. You also gonna need a number two like my man Chico here. Ain't that right Chico?"

"That is right, Terry."

"But hey, lil bro?" Terry went on. "Ya wanna keep the peace with them Screamin Ricans or waddever the fuck they called? You go meet with that Angel dude one on one. Layout ya shit and let em know you looking ta let bygones be bygones. Like ya looking ta share the street n shit. You know what I'm sayin? Do that before ya start sportin them colors and I guarantee you got an ally for life. Just make sure he know you ain't askin his permission, you just given him the respect to let him know what's gittin ready to go down. Am I correct Chico?"

"Correcto."

"You grasp lil' bro?"

Kasseem nodded.

"What about the flag," I asked.

Kasseem looked at me for a minute before the light went on.

"Oh yeah, the flag! Shit, I forgot about that mother fucker. Damn man."

"What? What flag y'all talkin bout?" Terry demanded, looking at me.

"There's this phantom kid they call 'spider.' He's a little guy. No more than five foot four, skinny with long black curly locks. Muthah fuckah can climb anything."

For an instant, I wondered if they called him spider because he could climb, or he could climb because his name was spider. I decided it didn't matter and went on with the explanation.

"So, this spider dude, he shimmies up the street light pole over on Frame Place, and he slides out on the arm, you know, that holds the light out over the street?"

"Yo Yo, hold up. Say what now? My man climbed up the metal assed light pole?" Terry was astounded.

The light pole was a straight-up metal structure about two stories high. It did have a sort of concave groove in it where a guy could put his sneaker, but I never saw anybody else who put his sneakers in there like spider did.

"Yeah man, that's what I'm tryin ta tell you. He climbed the muthah fuckin pole, shimmied out on the arm close up by where the light's at, and he hung that God damned flag."

"What God damned flag, God damn it?"

"The muthah fuckin Screamin Phantom flag," Kasseem finished the story.

"White boy's right, that shit's a problem," Terry re-stated the obvious.

"Y'all can't be havin that shit".

Country suggested we just take it down.

Terry had no shirt on under his vest. His chest seemed to pop out and his biceps rippled as he tensed at Country's suggestion.

"Take it down? Take it down. Man, you are one dumbass country simp. First off, who the fuck you got gonna scale that shiny assed beanstalk to go up and get at that flag? Huh? You can't be doing that shit any damn way unless you ready to fight. That's total disrespect boy. I ain't saying y'all can't take care-a yo selves or nothing, but I know scrappin ain't what y'alls about. Fightin with y'all neighbor is very bad fo biniss. Am I right Chico or am I wrong this time?"

Feeling Terry's sudden change in demeanor, Chico had instinctively adopted a defensive posture. He stepped back, with his right foot blading his body toward Country in the ludicrous possibility that Country might have been provoked to violence by Terry's demeaning remarks.

"Joo ain't never wrong meng," Chico replied without dimming his glare at Country.

"I heard that!" They did a double five slap and relaxed.

The chief Skell took another deep pull on the joint that had just come around his way again. He appeared very pleased with the fact that he was never wrong. Terry knew Chico was right about that because Chico was never wrong because he always agreed with Terry.

"So, what should we do about it?" Kasseem asked.

"You gonna hafta negotiate Pardnah. Awright? …Awright."

They went through some elaborate handshake.

"Now y'all get the fuck outta here. We got our own biniss to take care of. Y'all let me know if ya need anything else. We can't be fightin y'all's battles, but we can always supply some resources. Ya dig what I'm sayin?"

We dug. 'The Skells' had a lot of resources.

That was the end of the powwow. We went back to the B wing, told everybody what happened and formed 'The Family.' With the backing of the older Skells, we figured we would be alright. Kasseem was elected Prez and named his brother #2. But when it came to the shit about the flag, he asked me what I thought. We went down the hall and into the stairwell where the standpipe hose was. I told him I had a plan and laid it out for him. He told me it would never work and he stormed off talking some shit about a stupid assed crackah.

The problem with the flag was all about "face." The Screaming Phantoms had to save face. Angel had to save face. Taking the flag down was not going to happen. That would have meant disgrace to the click. Angel could never sell that. They would have beaten his balls off and somebody else would have emerged as the leader. Just the suggestion could have caused us all to go to war. Even worse, Angel was from the Bronx. He was part of the Screaming Phantoms on his old turf. Presumably, the uptown Prez gave him the green light to start the Flushing faction. If the Bronx got wind that 'The Family' persuaded Angel to take down the flag, they might have come down to Queens and assassinate him. That was a real possibility. I saw a couple of those boys pay him a visit once. They were the genuine article. Flushing was like the suburbs to those guys. They took a trip out to the country to visit their satellite crew. The "colors" were everything to a click, sacred like a Hindu cow. Putting the flag up there was probably a whim like graffiti. It was more of a stunt for the sticky-footed spider to enhance his rep. But once it was up there, it became so much more. It signified the Screaming Phantoms' right to exist. It was their deed to their turf. They had inadvertently staked their claim. No, that flag was not coming down. No way! No how!

So, what was Plan B? Putting 'The Family's' flag up on the same pole right next to theirs? Not a perfect plan. If you were part of a click, you were part of the *best* click. Your click had no equal. Make no mistake, clicks could coexist, but they weren't equal. 'Separate and unequal' was the mantra. If Angel agreed to put our colors on their pole, that would have been like saying that 'The Family' was just as good—just as cool, and just as bad as 'The

Screaming Phantoms.' It would also have said that 'The Screaming Phantoms' was just as good, just as cool, and just as bad as 'The Family.' Inevitably that would have led to dissension in the ranks of both sides. Problems for Angel and for Kasseem. Sooner or later, somebody would have torn the other guys' banner down and the shit would hit the fan. Bad idea for both sides of the street. I felt I had the perfect solution. Judging by his reaction, Kasseem didn't agree. Kasseem and Angel had the sit down. When he came back, our alpha dog was strutting big time.

"It's a done deal y'all. 'The Family' and 'The Phantoms' are tight and the flag is not gonna be a problem. Can I get it?"

Hand slapping went all around.

"Mother fuckah wouldn't roll at first. Hadda straighten his Rican ass out."

"So, what's gonna be with the flag?" somebody asked.

"Their boy, Spider's gonna hang our flag for us on our side of the street. It's gonna show that we good with them and they good with us. It's also gonna be like a warning to any other mother fuckahs who think they gonna come around here. They gonna have two God damned clicks to deal with!"

"You awright man," the praise came from his brother.

"There's one mo thing now y'all got to know. I offered Angel a little good faith."

The group grew immediately inquisitive. Kasseem had to play this one right.

"He didn't ask me for nuthin, ya understand. I just decided to put a little somethin out there to lock it uptight."

"What? What the fuck djoo put out there," Thumper demanded.

"A five percent discount on anything we sellin for one year to his crew."

"That's bull shit!" Country shouted. "I ain't doin it."

"See that's why we call you Country. 'Cause you got that hillbilly brain. This shit is good for us and I'm gonna tell y'all why, and you *are* gonna do it, and I just might not kick yo fuckin ass for contradicting me when I'm talkin."

Country was silent as Jose smacked the back of his head.

"This is why y'all made me Prez. Because I think of shit like this. First of all, we do this and they owe us big time. This ain't no pay off, ya dig? This ain't nuthin but a friendly gesture on our part that we may call on them spicks to repay down the road. It's a debt. Second, if they come around looking to cop somethin on discount, either raise the price or short the package. Just talk to me about it first. Nobody gets shorted without my approval, ya hear?"

No one would ever get the approval. We would have to eat five percent. Still, it was a pretty good deal and a brilliant idea. Everyone was satisfied and Kasseem had solidified his office with us and with 'The Phantoms.' When our meeting broke up, Kasseem pulled me to the side.

"That was a great fuckin idea about the flag, white boy. If anybody ever finds out it was yours I will kill your white ass."

That was as close to a compliment as I was going to get on this one.

Spider hung up the flag and we put together an alliance that would endure as long as the two clicks lasted. Now, we could fly the colors. In other words, you had to go out and get yourself a dungaree jacket and put 'The Family' on the back in iron-on letters. Then you could adorn the jacket with a variety of accouterments. Mine had a patch of Yosemite Sam on the shoulder because my nickname was Outlaw. I had another patch of Africa on a red, black, and green background to show my soulful solidarity, and a white shoelace through the buttonholes for no particular reason other than that I liked the way it looked. Sometimes, I would pin on a fur collar for special events. We wore those jackets every day.

Full dress Family colors.

THE TESTING PROCESS

Do unto others, then split.

"Vengeance is mine sayeth the Lord." But the Lord didn't grow up on New York City concrete. Every day brought a new test. Some were full out exams, while others were more like pop quizzes. A pop quiz could come up at any moment with a shove, or a look, or even a crack about your mother. You could let nothing slide. Every action had to bring on a reaction. Failure to react properly would result in some sort of immediate abuse and erosion of your rep. Extreme rep. erosion could result in revocation of your hangout card i.e. ex-communication from the click. So, I did what I had to do and I got my ass handed to me on more than one occasion. But I got hard and I didn't give up. Being the only white kid on the crew brought me more than my fair share of tests. As we got older, the tests became more serious.

I was always a lightweight and vulnerable to the pop quiz. Being hooked up with 'The Family' saved my butt many times and when some shit did go down, I didn't have to win, I just had to put up a respectable fight. I never was a real tough guy, so I took to carrying a broom handle around with me like a walking stick. Sometimes, it doesn't matter how bad you are, it's more about how bad people think you are. Publicly practicing stick tactics was a good idea. Nobody ever fucked with me when I had that stick, so I never had to use it. It wasn't always about fighting. There were other tests as well. Major exams came our way all the time. If somebody disrespected or hurt one of our crew, there had to be retribution. In the middle of a game of murderball in the B wing one afternoon, one of the building tenants started complaining. He opened his window and started yelling about his wife needing sleep. The woman was probably sick or having a problem, pregnancy, or something. We should have done the right thing and played somewhere else. We didn't. We cursed the guy out, blew him off, and kept on playing. After a while, the guy appeared with the building superintendent, Mr. Bracey. We thought Bracey was a nasty prick. He was about five foot nine and weighed close to three hundred pounds. Bracey wore blue jean overalls all the time and walked around angry all the time. He usually pushed a supermarket shopping cart. His favorite saying was, "This is a place to live in, not a barn."

The truth is, Bracey was doing his job. If he didn't do his job, he would have lost his job. So, this tenant got a hold of our ball and flipped it to Bracey. Then Bracey, like the high priest, drew his ceremonial screwdriver and sacrificed our ball before our eyes. This prompted a litany of commentary like "motherfucker this," "scumbag that," and "payback is a bitch." Well, the bitch paid back that night.

Once the sun retires, the demons go to work. One of the guys had a wrist-brace slingshot. The wrist-brace slingshot was not "your father's slingshot." This baby was made of metal and it had surgical tubing instead of rubber bands to launch rocks or marbles at a velocity readily capable of killing just about any living creature a boy might have encountered on the streets of Flushing. The accuracy was chilling. The rest of us just gathered rocks up on my garage roof. At an hour that most working family men, like our target, were sleeping, we crept up on that roof and launched our vengeance on the windows of the disgruntled tenant's ground floor apartment. Our grumpy complainant got a frightful wakeup call. His terrified wife probably told him to mind his business and start looking for another place to live. As for old man Bracey, he would have to repair the windows. It was kind of like killing two birds with one stone, except it was a whole bunch of stones.

Events like this were commonplace. Ronnie B. used to run with us for a while until he died of a heroin overdose. He drifted in and out of the click while he was off and on the smack. Ronnie was very tall for a kid. Probably six foot two, but he was very skinny. He was lanky. Ronnie lived in a two-bedroom apartment in the B-wing with his mother, his uncle who was also a heroin addict, and a bunch of brothers and sisters. Ronnie B. had some kind of beef with a kid from 41st Road. I don't remember what it was about, or if I even knew. Kasseem just grabbed me one day and said we had to take care of it. We took some cinderblocks up to the roof of the A wing. We followed Ronnie to the edge, he pointed out the kid's father's car, and we crushed it. Cinderblocks from seven stories can inflict a tremendous lot of damage. The entire car, roof, trunk, and hood were demolished. The kid's father hadn't done anything, but it was like a message. "Next time it will be your son's skull."

Shit like that could erupt at any moment. Not even the slightest hint of disrespect could be tolerated from anybody. There was no remorse and no empathy. I felt nothing for either of those poor families. It just seemed like the right thing to do at the time, another way to solidify my own rep, and a building block toward greater control of the neighborhood as we got older.

I needed all the rep I could muster. I was a white kid trying desperately and hopelessly to be black. I literally walked the walk, talked the talk, and dressed the part. But there was one thing I could not do. No matter how hard I tried, I couldn't change the color of my skin. Sure, I was part of a crew that looked at me as one of them, but other people didn't see me that way. Whenever the shit hit the fan, I was the first one to get smacked. Other white kids despised me and even the cops singled me out. From time to time, my pale face brought the heat down on 'The Family' that otherwise wouldn't have come. That was a big problem.

During the Disco era, disco roller skating became the rage. A rink opened up in Flushing Meadow Park at the scene of the 1964 World's Fair. It was called the 'Roller Round.' It was semi-indoors in the pavilion, with the two tall towers, with what appeared to be flying saucers on top. In the film *Men in Black,* these observation towers are revealed to contain the ships used by the first extraterrestrials to visit Earth. The World's Fair was organized to cover up the evidence of their landing. The 'Roller Round' was surrounded by twelve-foot walls, then it was open to the roof about a hundred feet above. For this reason, it was only operational in the warmer months. I have said it before, we weren't fighters per se. That wasn't our main goal. We were more about making money. But in the street, you better be ready to step up at any moment. If somebody fucks with one of your crew and you don't do anything about it, the whole click loses respect. If 'The Family' lost respect, we would have become a joke and we would have become vulnerable to other predators. The street is unforgiving and no one can be trusted. That's why I surrounded myself with brothers who would fight for me as long as I did the same for them. Loyalty is the only price for protection, and street cred is a powerful defense.

The 'Roller Round' was a pretty mellow spot. Every Wednesday night was 'soul night.' We just wanted to get high, do roller disco, meet girls, and sell reefer. The place was a wide-open market with no cops around. Security was strictly for fights and theft. Good times to be had, money to be made, and pretty much no heat! The problem was that out of maybe two to three hundred people, I was the only white kid. Not only that, but I had blondish hair. I was like a snowflake in a mud puddle. It was becoming a significant problem because we never knew when some shit might jump off. Somebody always got in my face, especially if I was with a black chick. The fellas spent the whole night looking after me. It got so bad that they actually asked me to stop going with them. Imagine how that made me feel. Reality check, "You are not black." I felt like dirt being white. I didn't want to fuck their good time, but I dug the atmosphere like they did and I really enjoyed skating. It was the only sport I was actually good at. I couldn't "ball" like the bruthahs on the court because white men can't jump. Handball wasn't my thing and I sucked at stickball. So, what could I do? I could skate my ass off. I had to come up with something.

I walked the walk. I talked the talk. I dressed the part. I just didn't look the look. There was no way to change that. The only thing I could do was to play down my whiteness. If I couldn't be black, maybe there was a way for me to be less white. I started wearing a hat. Sometimes it was a Fedora, sometimes a Kangol. With a little fuzz on my face and a hat hiding my hair, I could pass for Puerto Rican. I even spoke a little Spanish. Enough, at least, to pull off the charade. I went so far as to use some of that spray on wash out hair color to darken up the locks that spilled out from under the lid. It was a simple solution and it worked out okay. The problem of course was that under the façade, I was still white and I knew it. That reality was playing itself out in ways that would take me years to understand.

A TRAGIC PLACE

Every aspect of the pain, hopelessness, violence, poverty, and despair of our little piece of Earth was summed up in that one tragic event. That broken man was the soul of our turf.

He was Hispanic. Probably Puerto Rican. Many were. Maybe not. But he looked Puerto Rican, early thirties, and blitzed drunk. Now I don't mean to say that Puerto Ricans are drunks, because that may be how it sounds, but this Puerto Rican looking guy happened to be blitzed drunk. He was wearing a Guinea-tee, dress pants, and pointy demi-boots in a faux gator pattern. No socks. 'Guinea-tee' is what we called the sleeveless tank top. The Guinea-tee was soaked with blood that had obviously splattered from the gash on the face of the Puerto Rican looking guy himself. He was toting a bumper jack. Cars don't come with bumper jacks anymore. This was a three-foot-long piece of grey steel, with a nasty black ratcheting hook about three-quarters of the way down. That hook would insert smartly into a slot on a steel chrome bumper. The other end slipped into a tidy triangular base and, with the kind assistance of the tire iron, which was also used for popping the hub cap, even the most feminine of women could lift a Chrysler straight up off the ground, with a couple of serious pumps.

So, the guy was swinging this bumper jack like a Louisville Slugger and staggering up Sandford Avenue. Naturally, we followed. From across the street, we tailed this dude with great delight, hoping he would find the guy he was looking for. Speculation flew about what led up to the partial demolition of his face.

"Bet he caught some niggah fuckin his old lady. They prob'ly got into the shit and my man came up short."

"Bullshit man. That dude was getting busy with some other muthah fuckah's old lady, got busted, and got his Rican assed whipped."

The monologue went on as we moved up the street. All along it became apparent that the alcohol was catching up and our guy was running out of gas.

"All y'all way the hell off. This was gambling man. This muthah fuckah's up there shootin craps and getting all drunk. He's loosin all mama's Goya bean money. Ya dig what I'm saying? He startin to get pissed and starts snatching them dice. Next thing you know, some niggah comes off and yokes my man. Muchos tiempos. Am I right? Am I right?" We all slapped hands.

"Everybody now all intimidated and shit and the other dude scoops up the green and boogies on outta there. How about that shit? Now the muthah fuckah's out here gunnin for the man who stole his water."

The laughter was uproarious. But we stopped abruptly. It was like somebody made the "cut" sign. He was coming across the street. He must have heard us laughing. Holy shit that was one adrenaline cranking moment. There's three of us standing there. One minute we were laughing our asses off, and now we are watching this half-crazed, half-drunk, completely fucked up after getting his face bashed in, bumper jack swinging, wife-beater, bloody tee-shirt wearing, maybe Puerto Rican guy, coming our way and he is looking for somebody to beat on! What are we going to do? You can't be the first to run, but you damn sure don't want to be the first one crushed by that hook. We held.

Now, Sanford Avenue had a double yellow line painted down the middle and our guy was coming across from the other side and he was almost there. For a second, it looked like he was going to trip, but he didn't. I don't know what my boys were thinking, but I was hoping this dude would get creamed by a bus the minute his pointy faux-gator poked across the Mason Dixon.

It didn't happen. And he was bearing down on the line of parked cars between us and him. It wouldn't be long now. I was hoping somebody else would run, then we could all blast off and blame the runner later for punking out. Nobody bolted. Everybody held.

'*Shit! Here we go*,' I thought.

I can see him even now. His body twisted slightly as he slipped between a white Corvair and a T-Bird with suicide doors. The guy was in good shape. Not like Schwarzenegger, but more like James Cahn in the *Godfather*, and he was wearing a two-strapped brown leather wrist-band just above his left palm like 'The Sharks' in *West Side Story*. His butt rested a moment on the trunk lock of the T-Bird when he lost his balance. We each adopted our own defensive postures. He put one foot on the sidewalk. The crazy truth is that, at that moment, if he had turned to his right, he would have taken another wicked beating from a couple of frightened spectators watching his misery. Instead, he stumbled to his left and dragged his defeat toward the wall of another apartment building. A standpipe intake pushed out of the bricks of that building.

If you have ever been in the stairwell of a high-rise apartment house, you might have noticed a flaked fire hose, draped from metal thongs on each landing. Somewhere outside of the building, there would be an intake valve. That was called the standpipe system. In case of a fire, the firemen would hook their truck up to a fire hydrant, and hook a hose up to the standpipe intake valve. The truck would feed water to the hallway hose so the firemen could fight the fire on the upper floors. Actually, firemen don't trust those hallway hoses, so they carry their own hoses up the stairs and swap them out. There are a lot of reasons firemen don't trust the stairwell standpipe hoses, but one of them is because those hoses tend to accumulate a load of shit inside. We would stuff balls, fruit, toys, dead vermin, you name it, into those hoses. But the standpipe intake valve outside the building is also great to sit on. It was an amazing sight. This man hadn't simply been beaten by another man, he had also lost the battle of life. He stumbled to the standpipe, put his left hand on top, leaned forward, and laid that bumper jack down on the concrete. Then he went ahead and sat down slowly on the standpipe intake valve, and he slumped sadly forward like the crushed man that he was. He pressed his forearms into his thighs and hung his head between his legs. His thick black hair drooped and pointed to the ground. A single drop of blood splashed onto the sidewalk and he began to weep. We couldn't hear him but his bouncing shoulders said it all.

Every aspect of the pain, hopelessness, violence, poverty, and despair of our little piece of Earth was summed up in that one tragic event. That broken man was the soul of our turf. We were witnessing our own destinies. Remarkably, we were completely oblivious.

"Fuckin punk."

"I wudda shoved that jack straight up his faggot ass!"

"You got that shit right."

That broken man was sort of reincarnated for me one summer evening in Island Park. We got a call for a guy threatening people with a hammer. I got there before my partner in 421.

"C'mon out here muthah fuckah, I'll kill ya ass right here."

It was the local wino bugging out on his DTs again. He was clutching a basic claw hammer and he appeared to be menacing. I looked on until assistance arrived. Even a normally harmless old drunk can be dangerous in the wrong frame of mind.

"Stein again?" my partner asked.

They called the old man "Stein" because he used to have his own beer stein at the bar back when he could afford to drink at the bar.

"Yea, he's trippin," I replied.

"Let's just ship him. Did you call a bus?"

My partner wanted to send him to the mental ward and move on. The officer was on fill-in on 421's post. He would be gone tomorrow and Stein would be back tomorrow. Besides, the old wino needed help. He was probably somebody's father. I had a father with a drinking problem. And he reminded me of the Puerto Rican guy. That was my real motivation. I didn't share it.

"Let me see what's buggin him. Cover me."

"Are you fuckin kiddin me?" my partner was drawing his pistol as I walked toward Stein.

"Yo Stein, what's the ruckus? Who you yelling at?"

"That son of a bitch ran me out of my house. Now I'm gonna kill his fuckin ass."

"C'mon Stein, you're not gonna kill anybody. Lemme hold onto that hammer a minute and I'll help you bounce the son of a bitch."

My Partner had a bead on Stein as I reached cautiously for the hammer.

'Good thing it ain't a bumper jack,' I thought to myself.

"You gonna help me?"

"Sure," I nodded, "But you gotta let me hold that hammer for you."

The old drunk looked down at my hand, then he looked up into my eyes. He stared at me for a good while. He was trying to decide whether or not he could trust me. Then he laid the heavy end into my palm and I shoved the handle inside my gun belt.

"Okay, show me where he is."

We followed Stein behind a row of retail shops. He lived above the liquor store. How convenient. My partner holstered his weapon and shook his head as we walked.

"Yeah, he threw me out of my place and now he's runnin' hookers out of the joint."

I kind of hoped he was telling the truth. It could be a good bust. But I doubted his grip on reality. As we ascended the steps outside his apartment, my partner grabbed his arm so that I could go in first. We walked down a narrow hallway and entered a kitchen, living room, and bedroom all in one.

"There he is, on the couch," the drunk pointed at a weathered old pair of Levy's.

"He looks like a pair of jeans, but he's disguised," Stein slurred

I felt this man's pain. It was a pain that he would take to the grave. But I wasn't about to give up on him. Perhaps I could tranquilize that pain if only for a little while.

"Alright stand back," I gently guided Stein against the wall and away from the hallway we had just come from. "You," I shouted at the jeans, "Get up!"

I pulled my nightstick from the ring that hung it from my belt.

"I said get up!"

I struck the jeans. Then I did it again more ferociously.

"Get up and get the fuck outta here. Now, you son of a bitch!"

With the tip of my club, I slung the Levy's down the hallway toward the door. Then I kicked and cursed those pants all the way to the top of the steps, and with one final swift punt, I sent them to the sidewalk below.

"And don't you ever come back God damnit!"

When I turned back toward the room my partner was doubled over and trying very hard to control his hysteria. But Stein? Stein was awestruck. Someone had actually believed him and come to his aid. A huge burden had been lifted from him if only for one night. He put his hand on my shoulder and said, "Thank you, officer. Thank you."

Those simple words could not express the level of gratitude I read on his face. His sincerity was dumbfounding. A tremendous and rare sense of satisfaction came over me. It was like finding a lost child. Police work doesn't offer too many slaps on the back. A cop has to savor every one.

"You are one sick puppy," my partner said as we descended the stairs.

"You are not going to ruin this moment for me, my friend," I gloated.

Word got around the Precinct pretty quick and I took some abuse. But the guys genuinely admired what I had done. Even when Benzenberg came back from vacation, he mentioned it over coffee.

"I heard what you did for Stein. You are one crazy bastard, but you did good."

THE HILL

This was survival in that place. If I didn't throw these guys a couple of serious blows, I would find myself on the business end of those vicious antennas, and it would be my own people thrashing my ass.

We always had a beef with the boys from 'The Hill.' That's all I remember about it. Even before we became 'The Family,' we hated those guys and they hated us right back. 'The Hill' was just another click from down by the World's Fair grounds. They were a rough bunch of white boys and they hung out on top of this hill that every local kid used for sled riding. We called it 'suicide hill.' The boys from the hill area called themselves simply 'The Hill.' They were our natural enemies. It all stemmed from a little name-calling one afternoon in the snow and just kept rolling for years. Every time one of ours saw one of theirs, it was game-on. We tried to settle our differences once by playing a football game. What a great idea! Go up against an arch-rival in an unsupervised full-contact sport. I don't know who set up the event, but the guys and I found ourselves cobbling together helmets, pants, and jerseys from a myriad of sources. What we couldn't borrow, we boosted. By game day, we were pretty well outfitted. Of course, we had no grass where we hung out so we had to play in Flushing Meadow Park which was way too close to

Hill country. Bad move. We showed up on bikes. They showed up with spectators.

It took about three plays to get the blood boiling. Kasseem started complaining about getting cleated. He was wearing sneakers and a couple of the Hill boys had on baseball cleats which have sharp bottoms. When it happened again, Kasseem limped to the sideline and snatched up a fallen tree branch. I grabbed the guy closest to me as Kasseem broke that branch across the facemask of one of our adversaries. Then, an all-out brawl erupted as I slung my opponent to the ground. It's tough to hurt a guy who's wearing full protective gear, but there is a vulnerable spot just below the shoulder pads in the abdominal zone. I found that spot on one guy and then another before I took a block in the back sending me sprawling.

Everybody was duking it out. When you watch big fights like this on television, the hero always seems to have an owl vision. The reality is that when the adrenaline begins to pump, the focus narrows. As I rolled over, I saw a cleat coming at my face. I grabbed that shoe and leaped to my feet, temporarily dumping my attacker. This gave me an instant to take a quick survey of the melee. I saw a couple of guys had taken their helmets off. *'That's pretty risky,'* I thought as I spotted the guy I dumped scrambling my way. I began to turn my focus back to him when suddenly the sound of an airhorn pierced the air. There was fighting going on all over the field and many of the spectators had jumped in. Every head turned toward the backside of the park to see a souped-up, Chevy, hot-rod raising a cloud of dust, as it barreled across the grass in our collective direction. The driver was laying on that airhorn and it seemed as if the action completely froze for an instant before everyone bolted at the realization that the Chevy wasn't going to stop.

I didn't turn around until I got to the Van Wycke Expressway overpass. I heard Ronnie B. yelling, "Yo, Kev."

I turned as he came up alongside on a bike. I had left mine behind. No problem, I would steal another.

"Jump on."

He rode us back to the B-wing. Some of the guys were there. Others showed up later with tales of minor aftershocks on the way home. That was our last attempt at any civil exchanges with 'The Hill.'

Not long after, on a late fall afternoon, I was walking down Frame Place. Frame Place was a side street that intersected Sanford Avenue at the corner of my apartment building. That's where our flag, and 'The Phantoms' flag, were flapping in the wind. All of a sudden, Thumper says, "Yo, that muthah fuckah's from 'The Hill,'" pointing toward a kid walking on the other side of the street in the opposite direction.

What balls! Here's this Hill boy, walking right down our street, without paying a toll.

"Whadda you looking at muthah fuckah," I yelled.

With that, he pulled out a black pistol and leveled it in our direction.

"Oh shit!" we dove behind the parked cars. There was a muffled "pop" and when we peaked out. Hill boy was halfway up the street and still running.

"You hit," Thumper gasped pointing at the right side of my nose.

"Damn," I said as I gazed at the blood on my finger, having touched it directly to the spot he was looking at.

"He's gonna pay for this."

I only got a glimpse of the piece, but it looked like a .45 caliber semi-automatic handgun. Obviously, it wasn't a .45, or my whole face would have been blown off. The blood was just a trickle and what I guessed had been a pellet must have bounced off, or so I thought.

Fast forward. It's twelve years later and I'm running down Austin Blvd. on my post in Island Park. I was in foot pursuit of a fleeing warrant suspect. I was right on his ass when he dashed into the Great Bear Automotive Repair Shop. With me in hot pursuit, he darted through the shop and a doorway into the clean part of the building. A frightened clerical woman ran out screaming, as he came to a dead-end in the back of the shop's office. When I went to grab him, he picked up a telephone off the desk and hit me in the side of the head with it. Cell phones were still on the drawing board and this was no little cordless. It was an old-fashioned, hard-wired black desktop phone, with the pigtail receiver and a rotary dial. It weighed about two pounds and it dazed me. The guy was a small-time local petty hood. He had a habit of ignoring his moving violation tickets so he would pop warrants on a regular basis. That's when I liked to grab him. Sometimes, he'd give up some information in exchange for a free ride. Other times, he'd turn up dirty with some reefer or a weapon. That's when I could really squeeze him. If he didn't come across with some really solid intel or agree to do a buy on somebody, he'd be collared. This time he was coming in. I got in a shot of my own and I cuffed the guy up after a short struggle. He took a few lumps in the process, so the prisoner and I wound up at the same hospital from where we were both "treated and released." His diagnosis was minor abrasions and contusions. Mine was a slight concussion.

"So how long have you had that pellet in your face," the doctor asked.

"Pellet? I don't know about any pellet."

"Here, I'll show you the x-rays."

The white-coated, young resident slid two celluloid snapshots up into the clips on the wall. When he flipped on the light behind them, there it was; a perfect little sphere, lodged in my upper jaw, just below my right nostril and right above the top of the roots of my teeth.

'*Son of a bitch,*' I thought back ...

"That son of a bitch is gotta pay for this shit," Kasseem blared. "How come you didn't catch that muthah fuckah?"

"He was too far," I said. "Besides, he was shootin at us!"

"I should whip both your asses for letting him get away on our God damn street! First chance we get, we gonna lure his crackah ass in behind the Turk's."

The superintendent of the building, on the other side of the street, was Turkish and so we called it the Turk's building. He had two kids, a son named Attila, and a girl named Nur. I guess he was looking for a better life for them. The Turk's was like the Little Bighorn. You could go through a gate on Frame Place and walk behind the building along a fenced-in area. Straight ahead was a fifteen-foot wall that was the side of the garage of Jose's building. That fence was there long before Jose's building was built. The Turk's was a grand old structure, with an opulent lobby and some fabulous architecture. I didn't appreciate any of that then. When you reached the wall, you could turn right and walk in the canyon between Jose's building and the Turk's. A stairway led down to an ally cut out of the first floor of the Turk's, and the ally opened into an airshaft between the buildings. One way in, same way out, and no windows. We called it 'the rat-trap'. A rat is a wily creature. He is lightning quick and so flexible that he can get in and out of spaces much smaller than his own body. Rat's are almost impossible to catch. This spot was so tight, even a rat couldn't escape, figuratively speaking.

It was about two weeks before the next Hill boy sighting. I think it was Ballah who spotted them on Sanford up by Main Street. He breathlessly told us of their approach as he had run all the way. There were two of them. No problem. The plan was that I would lure them into the ambush in the rat trap. Everybody knew what to do, we had already planned it. There was no need for more than a 'let's do it,' before we sprang into action. I set off to do my act. Behind me, the boys would be snapping off car antennas on their way to the ambush site. Automobile radio antennas made a handy weapon for decades. They stood rigid upright from the hood of the front passenger's side of just about every car on the road at the time. The average antenna collapsed down to about eight inches in height but could telescope out to as much as three feet for optimal radio reception. Easily torn away from the vehicle, they were always accessible when you needed to make a point. We were about to do a whole dissertation.

I found my prey just around the corner and across the street. With a simple "Yo faggots, you want some of this?" they took the bait.

I bolted and they followed. If they caught me before I made it to the jump site, I would have been the one in trouble. It would take a while before my homies realized something was wrong and came looking for me. In the meantime, there were two of them and one of me; I'd have to hold my own. On the other hand, if I got too far out in front, they might just give up on me and quit the chase. I had to play this one just right. It was one full block to the first turn through the gate; from there it was a short sprint to the wall, the last turn, a six or seven-step plunge under the building, through the alley, and into a swamp of ass-kicking. My pulse was cranking with fear and exhilaration. It would all dissolve into remorse before that day ended. Halfway down Frame Place, I jerked my head around to see them right where I wanted them to be. The gate was open when I burst into the Turk's yard. Slowing slightly at the wall, I let them close in. Then down the steps, we bound. They must have thought I was some kind of sucker to put myself in a box in my own neighborhood. '*Who's the sucker now, Hill boys?*' I thought as the whipping began. The car antennas tore through their clothing and welted their faces. There were probably five of us, maybe six, raising Hollywood terror in their astonished eyes. My regret mounted as the fists and feet began to fly. Some of the others appeared to be enjoying the slaughter. A couple of my boys were very angry and very dangerous people. They delighted in inflicting pain. The rest of us were duty-bound. I knew what this was going to be. There was no surprise. There was no shock. How could I have let that happen to those boys? It was the law of the lawless. Hurt or be hurt.

"They've had enough!" I blurted, followed by a few 'Are you shittin' me? This muthah fuckah just shot you in the face' looks.

Of course, they hadn't had enough. I would have to take my shots. This was survival in that place. If I didn't throw these guys a couple of serious blows, I could find myself on the business end of those vicious antennae, and it would be my own people thrashing my ass. My Family would beat me severely for punking out and then I would be expelled. I'd be on my own again, and fighting every day.

The shooter was already on the ground writhing in pain and hoping the onslaught had ended. He saw me approaching and he knew what was coming. His eyes pleaded but his mind knew it was useless. He grew up on the same streets with the same rules. That boy knew what I had to do, just as he himself would if it were me groveling on that pavement. Two kicks to the gut were delivered before I put the Converse All-star imprint on the side of his face. The other kid was far less pathetic. Two of my guys were holding him upright, and a third took him by the hair from behind. This dude had a Sylvester Stallone thing going on. His face said, 'Whatever don't kill me, makes me stronger.' He gave me some motivation when he asked, "What you got punk?" He was a true badass. Bleeding, and obviously, in pain, he wasn't showing a glimpse of the fear he must have felt. He would rather have died first. Suddenly, I remembered why we were there and I brought one up from down south. It was like that one perfect swing. I was never a long ball hitter, but one warm spring afternoon, I caught one on the sweet spot and sent it over the left-field fence and onto the roof of the park house at P.S. 20. That was my best hit ever. And now, this was my long ball, probably the single best punch I ever delivered that drove this guy's jawbone skyward and sent him sprawling. A quick toss of their pockets reaped a rolled-up Marvel comic book, a handful of 'Man From Uncle' trading cards, two bags of M&Ms, a 007 gravity knife, about fifteen bucks cash, and a dime bag of pot.

There are a lot of things I've done in this life that I'm ashamed of, but few that I truly regret. Those are the character-defining choices for which there were alternative selections to be made without altering my destiny. One of those events was my failure to say goodbye to the girl I was loving when I met my wife. Another was grabbing a drunk for DWI the night he buried his mother. The savage beating of those kids is my earliest memorable regret. On my run to bait them, I had a fleeting impulse to not find them. No one would ever have known the truth, but something drove me forward. Maybe it was momentum, maybe payback. In any case, it was a tragic decision that still haunts my nights, even though they both walked away from it.

Robazz on the left and Kasseem on the right. Robazz is a barber by trade.
The little photo is of Robazz when he was about 6.

BUSTED IN THE BRONX

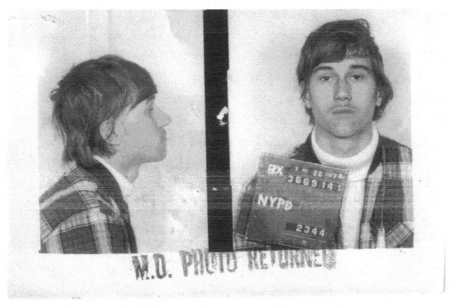

Kick that butt over here, faggot!

Marijuana and cocaine were plentiful and seemed perpetually available on a local basis. If I didn't have it, somebody else did. Either that or together we knew where to find it without too much effort. Not that we were doing coke that much. It was way more expensive than the reefer, and the head was too short. Like a good stand-up comic, cocaine always left you wanting more. The more exotic stuff like touies, bennies, black beauties, hashish, and hallucinogens was a lot tougher to find. Every now and then, the neighborhood would cough up something out of the ordinary, but if we or a client wanted to cop something special on a particular day, that would probably require some travel.

There was this White guy I knew in the Bronx named Archie. It was usually a white guy who had the 'off the wall' kind of shit. I have no recollection of how I came to know Archie. All I remember is that I had his number in my little black pocket phone book and he was a good source for a couple of hits of THC every here and there. I would call Archie from some payphone booth in 212. If he had the THC, I would take a ride up there and score. If he didn't, he would tell me when I might call back and check. Archie ran his modest business out of a school yard somewhere off of the Cross Bronx Expressway. I used to drive up there in my father's orange Mustang. I'd park the car, meet the guy, do the deal, get back in the car, and come home. The toll on the Whitestone Bridge was only a quarter. Most of the time somebody would come with me, more for the company than for security. I trusted Archie and, even though it was the Bronx, it felt pretty safe. The fact is, the purchase was for personal use. We weren't moving any weight. I never copped more than three or four hits off of the guy, so there wasn't enough money to attract a shakedown. Plus, we were going to his place of business. That's where he worked every day. The chances of a double-cross here were low on both sides.

And so, it started out one January morning in 1974. I called Archie looking to score some THC. The payphone rang about seven times. He eventually picked up and said he didn't have any but, "By the way, I got a shitload of blotter acid."

Acid, of course, is LSD (Lysergic acid diethylamide). LSD came in three forms that I knew of. There was liquid acid that you could ingest directly, put on a sugar cube, or insert via an eyedropper, straight into your eye socket. Acid also came in a tiny little pill that I only remember seeing in purple. It was called Purple Haze. Jimmy Hendricks made that shit famous with the song of the same name. Finally, there was Blotter acid or just plain 'Blotter.' Blotter came in sheets of paper with a checkerboard design. Each box on the checkerboard had a drop of acid-soaked into it. How much acid? Who the fuck knows! That's why I never did any acid. It very likely caused irreparable brain damage every time you took it.

Despite the fact that I didn't use it, I loved to sell it. You could get about one hundred hits for around eighty bucks, and sell them for $2.50 - $3 each. Without personal consumption, the first thirty-five got you your investment back, and the other sixty-five were pure profit. So, when old Arch said he had a shitload, I heard opportunity knocking. We made a deal over the phone for five-hundred hits for $375. That would be about twenty sheets of Blotter. The only problem was that Archie didn't want to do the deal in the schoolyard. He thought it was too hot for a caper like this. The schoolyard was his turf, so I figured he knew best about what was what, but I was a little suspicious. You had to learn to trust your instincts. I happened to have gotten beat on an acid deal once before, and I wasn't about to walk into a setup, especially way up there in the Bronx. But I wanted this stuff, so I went along and asked where he had in mind to do it. His answer really surprised me.

"The Bronx Zoo."

"The mother fucking Bronx Zoo?" I exclaimed. "That's beautiful man!"

And it was a beautiful plan, or so it seemed. I figured there would be no cops and no chance of getting popped. There'd be lots of people on a Saturday afternoon in autumn, so there'd be little to no chance of getting robbed. And we could blend in and slip off to a public restroom somewhere and get it done. Plus, I loved the zoo! Bonus! We set it up.

Of course, I was no chump. Even though it sounded nice and neat, three hundred and seventy-five bucks was a lot of green to me. I wasn't planning on leaving that park without my drugs or my money, one way or the other. I was going in armed. I didn't bring a gun, but I did bring a weapon. I also brought two guys with me, Tookie and Satch. Tookie was a good choice. Because he wore those glasses, people tended to underestimate him. That was a mistake. He was a pretty tough dude and he wouldn't back down from a fight. When things started getting hot, Tookie would slowly take off his glasses and put them carefully into his pocket. If possible, he would make sure that the other guy caught him doing it. It was a calculated and intimidating move. It said, "Hey, I'm ready to go." Satch was big and scary looking. He had a face that could only be improved by a good beating. But Satch was a bit of a pussy and he would give up his mother if he thought it would save his ass. I was letting it all ride on the bluff, hoping the other guys would judge the book by the cover.

Satch didn't hang out with us on a regular basis. He wasn't in 'The Family.' Satch, however, had something else going for him. His aunt was stashing pot in her apartment for her boyfriend who was dealing in weight. I'm talking about pounds. The guy was moving a lot of reefer. He had a rapid turnover. The smoke moved through there so quickly, that he never caught on that Satch was tapping the stash. Satch never got greedy and for a few months there, we had a great run on the boyfriend's dime. We stayed high Sun to Sun until he got busted.

While I was a detective sergeant, I got involved in a raid on a marijuana dealer. It started when we grabbed a small timer doing a hashish deal in a bank parking lot. The teller spotted some suspicious activity from the drive-through window and called 911. When the uniformed officers got to the scene, the dealer had already left in his BMW convertible, but the teller had the plate number. The cops grabbed the buyer, who was still in the parking lot, and he sang like Elvis. He had about 1/2 ounce of hash on him and he gave up the whole deal, including the dealer's name and description, right on the spot. The plate on the BMW came back to a yogurt parlor on the north shore. Detective P.J. Clark caught the case. PJ and I took a ride up there and we took the uniformed cop with us. It was the same cop who first busted the buyer in the bank parking lot. It was a pat on the back for the officer, and it was always nice to have a uniform nearby. I went into the yogurt shop alone first, just to scout it out. The dealer was in there just as described, and he was by himself. He came out of a little quasi-office kind of room in the back to serve me my desert. I caught a glimpse of a stack of cash on the desk as he shut the door behind him. I ordered a small strawberry yogurt with toasted coconut on top, paid him, and left.

After I finished my treat, P.J. dropped the uniformed cop and me off a couple of doors down from the entrance and drove around to cover the back door. As soon as he radioed that he was in place, the cop and I went in. There was no one else in the place and the guy offered no resistance in the face of our drawn guns. I let the police officer cuff him up as a reward for the job he did back at the bank. When I was working the street, the squad dicks used to push the cops aside and steal the show. I decided I would never do that if I made detective and I never did.

Detective Clark came in through the back and I directed him to scoop up all the cash. There was a lot of cash. He sure didn't make all that dough selling frozen desserts. I flipped the "YES WE'RE OPEN" sign around to "SORRY WE'RE CLOSED" before locking the front and back doors with the guy's keys. P.J. and the officer transported the suspect back to the station house. I dropped the top on the Beamer and transported the car. The detective and the cop took the money. If I was alone with the cash, that could have led to allegations.

Back at the squad, and after PJ gave him his Miranda warnings, our collar gave us written consent to search his house. Det. Clark stayed behind to book the perp. He also notified the narcotics squad and the asset forfeiture squad because we had seized a pile of money and a sporty little BMW. I took a small team out to the yogurt boy's house. His wife was surprised to see us. We had unlimited consent to search the entire house. I still can't believe the wife didn't call a lawyer. She just stepped back and let us go in it. I guess she figured that day might come and she just sort of resigned herself to the inevitability of it. The search didn't turn up any more drugs, but we did find a small-caliber semi-automatic handgun and a photo of our perp getting a blow job from some woman who wasn't his wife. That would prove to be a sweet little bargaining chip when it came to asking our boy for a favor.

When we got back to the station house, the Narcs were busy grilling yogurt boy about his connections. The lead detective was a pony-tailed, hippie-looking dude named Tony Dobies. Tony had been a first-rate street cop before he was asked to join the department's newly formed crack team sometime around 1985. By this time, he was a well-seasoned narcotics detective, and a great guy to have on the case. The problem was that our collar decided that he had given us enough and he wasn't rolling over on his source.

I grabbed Tony on the side and showed him the snapshot of the wannabe porn star yogurt boy. At my suggestion, Tony took the photo back into the interrogation room to ask the dealer if his wife was acquainted with the babe in the photo. Ten minutes later, he gave up his connection and we were orchestrating a controlled phone call. That's where the bad guy gave us written consent to record the call between him and his supplier. You can imagine our glee when the guy on the other end agreed to sell his client a pound of pot that very night!

"It's your lucky day man. I just got a brand-new shipment this morning. When can you get here?"

"One hour," I mouthed to yogurt boy.

"One hour," he spat into the phone.

Quickly, we assembled a squad of plain-clothed cops, detectives, and a battering ram. There was no time to muster up a SWAT team. Our schedule was too tight. We mounted up in three cars and headed out to Manhattan. I didn't think that we could take a collar out of New York City and bring him back to Nassau, but detective Dobies assured me that it could be done based on a criminal enterprise charge. That was good enough for me.

Yogurt boy turned informant and took Tony D right into the guy's apartment. It was risky because Tony wasn't wearing a wire, but he promised me that he would stay close to the door and let us in if things went bad. Despite his word, we squatted outside the apartment with an ear to the keyhole, and the battering ram poised and ready to unhinge the steel door. The instant the deal was done, Tony opened the door and we rushed in. The city dealer actually put up a little scuffle. I think he was just showing off for his girlfriend who was there, cuffed on the couch, watching. She was an attractive Asian woman with eyes as wide as tea saucers. She obviously had not bargained for this. Three of the undercovers were wearing masks to conceal their faces, but they looked like medieval executioners. They were very frightening.

I've never seen so much marijuana in one place before or since. When we began carrying the pounds out by the box full, all of the local kids gathered on the sidewalk hoping we would drop some. They knew who we had grabbed and they knew what we were hauling. When I looked at them, and they were all yelling something about leaving a little taste or letting them guard the apartment, it flashed me back to about seventeen years ago.

"Yo Office-ah, you need us to help you carry anything," I shouted from the crowd as the NYPD dragged that dealer out of Satch's aunt's apartment with all that marijuana. Right behind him, came Satch's aunt all cuffed up. The party was over. The faucet was turned off and I wanted to cry. But that was after the incident at the zoo.

So, off we drove to the Bronx; Tookie, Satch, and me, all blown out of our shorts on the snatch from Satch's aunt's boyfriend's stash. The plan was to meet "where the antelope play." I guess Archie was a bit of a poet. There was a fenced-in area where the zoo housed a variety of roaming deer species and antelopes were among them. My team and I got there about a half-hour ahead of schedule to scope it out. The deer cage was easy enough to find and everything looked cool. Needless to say, it wasn't the most popular exhibit, so there weren't too many people around. We had some time to kill, so what do you suppose we did?

"Time to get high bruthahs."

Being stoned and doing a drug deal was probably not a wise move. This proved to be far more consequential than I could have imagined. Satch whipped out the reefer or the "chiba-chiba," as he called it, and began rolling. Unfortunately, the process was interrupted by the hum of a Honda. Satch instinctively released the pot and it fell to the ground. But it was too late. The scooter cop had already seen it. Who knew there were cops on scooters patrolling the Bronx zoo? In hindsight, and knowing what I now know about police work and police officers, the last thing this cop probably wanted was to get involved in a bullshit arrest and ruin his day. He had a nice, quiet detail in the park and I'm guessing he had dinner plans.

"Pick that shit up," he demanded. "I saw you drop it. You know smoking marijuana in public is a serious crime?"

He then turned to Tookie. Tookie had an Afro pick sticking out of his hair. It was big and made of metal. It resembled a pitchfork.

"What's this?" the officer questioned as he plucked it out. Tookie's response was not well thought out.

"It's a comb. Is that illegal too?"

'Uh oh,' I thought, 'We're fucked now.'

"Okay, wise ass. Hands on the fence. This is blah blah to central K," he blurted into his mike. "Request assistance with three suspects," and he gave his location.

It was frisk time and I was armed.

'Good thing we didn't hook up with Archie yet,' I thought. Five hundred hits of Blotter would have been a definite trip to Rikers Island. I still had a chance to skate.

"Why are you harassing us," I heard Tookie say as the officer put his hand on my weapon, a set of chukka sticks. I didn't even know they were illegal.

"Shut the fuck up man," I shouted at Tookie.

It was too late. The cop was pissed and the cuffs went on. This was going to be my first 'big boy' arrest. I'd been brought in several times as a juvenile, but now that I was seventeen, this could mean a trip to the men's house, and I was not happy. Tookie got cut loose because he was clean. I couldn't help thinking that his big mouth played a huge roll in what, for me, was going to be about sixty-eight hours in police custody. Satch wound up getting a desk appearance ticket and a ride home from his older brother who was obviously annoyed at having to make the trip uptown. I wasn't eligible for a ticket based on my offense. I got a ride to Bronx central booking in a Paddy wagon. That's old Irish slang for the prisoner van.

The arrest processing took several hours. The scooter cop had handed me off to a detective. At some point, I remember being outside of a rustic old station house that probably once housed some aristocratic Bronx family. There were trees and ivy-covered walls. I was being watched by two uniformed officers while the detective went inside for a minute. One of them took his gun out and pointed it at my feet. He said, "You look like a nigger. You know how to dance like one?"

Perhaps it was not odd at all that I felt good about that. I was complimented and rewarded that he had noticed how much I resembled the brothers I hung out with. The four-inch Smith and Wesson revolver bearing down on my toes didn't faze me in the least. I knew that asshole wasn't going to shoot me in the parking lot of the Precinct. He had confirmed for me that I was close to achieving my goal of fitting in. My detective was not at all amused.

"Don't you point your fuckin gun at my prisoner? What's the matter with you?"

He took hold of my arm and led me inside to a desk and a typewriter. It is remarkable how little the process evolved over the next twenty years. It still takes forever to crank out the paperwork.

When we were done, I got tossed in the paddy wagon with a few other guests of the city and we made the rounds. The wagon stopped several times to pick up other prisoners around the Borough. There were some hard-assed criminals in on that ride. When I got to Central Booking, I don't mind saying it now, I was scared shitless. They took the cuffs off me and ushered me into the 'bullpen.' The bullpen was a huge, open cage filled with the recently arrested. There were three cement block walls; one in the back, and one along each side. The front was all bars. One lone, silver metal toilet stood in the back corner exposed to all. My first thought was, "God, please don't let me have to take a shit." God heard me.

As the turnkey officer opened the only gate to allow me to enter, I noticed a bald, white guy talking to one of the guards through the bars. Baldy was a sharp dresser. He had on a mocha-colored, three-quarter leather jacket, with a pair of demi-boots to match, a nice open-collared button-down shirt and a pair of jeans with a razorblade crease ironed in. I guessed he had shaved his head to blend in. Much the same as I had done to hide my white boy hair with hats. My choice for the Bronx foray was a Skimmer. The Skimmer was a ridiculous Beefeater/Amish style knit hat with a circular brim. It was crocheted, so I had to put cardboard inside the brim to keep it flexed. Naturally, it had been taken away from me and invoiced with my property now; however not without leaving its mark. I had a very serious case of hat hair. Coupled with my weak go-tee, it made me look a little tougher. As a skinny little cracker in this place, I needed every edge.

So, this guy Baldy, he was really cool man. This was the guy I wanted to be, standing up there with one foot on the bars, smoking a cigarette and bullshitting with the guards like he knew them. In fact, I think he did.

"C'mon Edward," the guard said in a 'give me a fuckin break' kind of way, "You're a professional con. Go sell your shit somewhere else."

The guard walked away. Eddie turned with his eyes toward the floor and then he glanced my way as the gate slammed shut behind me. His eyes told me to get out now. "Don't wind up like me," is what they said. I didn't listen.

There were a few wooden benches around the pen. They were bolted to the floor so they couldn't be moved or used to crush another prisoner. I copped a squat, that is, I sat down on one of them and began carefully observing the goings-on. My best strategy, I thought, was to keep to myself for now. Avoid eye contact and try not to talk to anybody. A couple of guys inquired about what I was "in for." "Gun," I said to one. "Shot somebody," I said to another. Like a fish story, my crime got more serious as time went on. I had to make them think I was a bad-ass and not to be fucked with. I didn't ask them any questions and eventually, they went away.

There was an emaciated, old, white man standing on the other side of the bullpen. He appeared to be a derelict. His head was losing its hair in an odd and uneven pattern. No razor had touched his face in quite some time, but his beard was not kempt. In fact, it resembled bramble. There were about three inches between the tops of his filthy sneakers to the bottoms of his high-water slacks, yet the waist was far too big. He stood there, clutching his belt loops to keep his pants from dropping to the floor. No one was permitted to have a belt or shoelaces. I guessed that his belt had been a length of rope and that the cops had probably been forced to cut away his laces due to all of the repair knots from breakage between the eyelets. Smoking was still permitted in jail, at that time, and the old geezer's eyes continuously scanned the concrete for any butts with unused smoking time on them. When he'd spot one, he would drag himself over to it, bend down, pick it up, pop it between his teeth, and fire it up from a book of matches in his torn shirt pocket. Those butts had been sucked on and stepped on by some of the scurviest people I had ever seen in one place. The old derelict had obviously smoked worse. It took three officers to deposit our next guest. The guy was clearly a local Latino. The Bronx had led him to drugs and he looked older than he probably was. Still, he did not come quietly. He was scuffling and rowdy all the way down the hallway, so much that it prompted many to be distracted to the bars to get a preview of what was coming our way. I kept my seat as the guards heaved him through the gate. The new guy gave the bars one last kick before turning completely calm. It was all pretty much an act.

"Yo, what's happenin fellas," he addressed the room in general. He glanced around the pen as he took a slow lap.

Probably looking for somebody he knows, I thought.

Then, to my utter amazement, he put his foot up on one of the benches, reached into his sock, and extracted three glassine envelopes filled with heroin. I knew it was heroin because nothing else came packaged in that way. In fact, I don't think those glassine envelopes were used for or made for, anything else besides packaging heroin. Maybe collectible stamps.

So, this junkie brakes out these three baggies of dope, tears one open, pours it out onto that flat spot on his fist between the base of his thumb knuckle and the base of his pointer finger knuckle, and snorts it up right there in front of whomever happened to be watching. Then he rips into bag number two and he does the same thing. Only this time, he uses his other nostril. Of course, the guys got only two nostrils, so he turns toward the room and says, "Hey! Anybody wanna ride the horse one mo' time before goin off to da group home?" Some guy jumped right on it and there went the contents of glassine envelope number three directly into his sinus cavities. Then they both plopped down on the bench just as the guard sauntered by. They'd be numb for the night.

Meanwhile, across the room, the old geezer's legs got tired of holding him up. He was on the edge of the bench with his elbows on his knees. His chinos were no longer in danger of falling off, so he was able to focus his radar on scanning the floor for cigarette butts. This was his way of passing time.

Suddenly, his eyes captured a fairly good-sized smoke someone had discarded somewhat prematurely for the lockup, where rations would be scarce for a while.

"Hey you!" the crazy bastard shouted, "Yeah you in the black jacket. Kick that butt over here faggot."

The bullpen was noisy like a baseball game, but suddenly it became quiet as a church when that very large black man, and his extra-large black leather motorcycle jacket, turned and glared at the hobo.

He practically whispered but the place was so quiet now that everyone could hear.

"What did you say to me?"

"You heard what I said. Kick that fucking butt my way ya faggot. I don't feel like getting up," the old man exclaimed.

As the biker moved in his direction, the geezer showed no fear, even though his neck was surely about to be snapped. Other men just stepped back and let the big guy slide slowly in the direction of the doomed old man. Although I never spoke to anyone in that pen about this, I am certain that each and every thief, druggie, rapist, and killer in that joint was as astonished as I was when the old man's executioner took out a pack of cigarettes, slid one from the box and said, "Here you go, man. Have a virgin." He then stuck it in the guy's mouth and lit it for him.

The deranged old fool took a long draw on that, exhaled, and spouted, "Don't think this makes me your bitch."

The giant cage exploded into uproarious hilarity that echoed around for several minutes. There were guys rubbing tears from their eyes and the guards didn't have a clue why.

"What the hell's so funny," one officer demanded.

"Your mother's twat," was the anonymous reply.

More laughter followed. Everyone in the pen was in on the joke. Everyone that is, except for the dope sniffing junkies. Those two were long gone in their zone and into a deep nod.

Dope fiends were famous for 'nodding out.' Now, heroin usage is a terrible American tragedy. I lost several friends to the 'white horse' and I certainly don't mean to make light of the plight of an addict. But with twenty to thirty hours to kill in the Bronx Central Booking, watching a couple of nodding junkies can be an amusing pastime. The best way I can describe it is like a person slipping into a coma in slow motion while sitting up. First, the guy's eyeballs roll back in his head. Then, his eyelids begin to droop until they're so close to closed that you could just about swipe a credit card through the slit. Next, his bottom lip drops open and his head slowly begins to droop. It goes down, down, down, and when his chin falls just beneath his nipples, his head pops up like a driver dozing off at the wheel. But his eyes never fully open and the process begins again. Down, down, down. By now, a little drool may begin oozing out of the corner of his mouth. Maybe he will take a drag off his smoke or maybe he will forget he is smoking at all. The cigarette might just burn right through his fingers. It was not uncommon to see heroin addicts with burn marks between their pointer and middle fingers, the slot most commonly used to clutch the little cancer sticks.

The antics of these two characters proved to be most entertaining. It began with the normal routine. It was like synchronized nodding. One head went down and the other popped up as two puddles of spit began growing on the floor at their feet. The guy who snorted the two bags kept slipping off the bench. He would catch himself with a stomp, get repositioned, and then go back into his nod. I imagined two bowls of soup on a table in front of them and their faces slowly sinking below the surface. By that time, neither of them knew where they were, or why, and perhaps more significantly, neither one cared. The real show was about to start. The junkie sitting on the left kept trying to put his feet up on the bench next to him, but the bench was just a few inches too far away for him to reach. He would lock out his legs until the balls of his feet just rested against the side of the bench. Then he would commence his nod. Just as his chin started to drop, his sneakers slipped off the bench, and his heels crashed to the concrete floor jolting him out of his trance.

Then, he leaned forward, grabbed the wooden slab, and vainly tried to drag it closer to him. Of course, the bench was bolted to the ground. But my man here would not be persuaded. He grabbed the short side of that bench and tugged on it with all of his dope smothered heart. Once he was convinced it was close enough, he went ahead and plopped the balls of his dingy Pro-Keds back up, on the corner of the pine, and went back into that junkie nod until his feet dropped to the ground again. Then, he went back and started tugging on that bench just like it was a brand-new day in the garden. In his inebriated state, that fucking seat moved and he tried again to get himself comfy in the man-cage. Once again, he failed. This display continued three or four times until some beast walked over and whacked the doper in the back of his head.

"That fuckin bench don't move dumbass! Stop yankin on it like some damn fool asshole!"

I'm not convinced that the junkie really understood why he just got smacked, but I sure as hell knew one thing for certain, I wasn't in Kansas anymore. This was the real deal, and I had no homies in the Bronx. I was a skinny little white boy, pretending to be black in a very dangerous place where race was a man's ID card. Blacks wouldn't have me because I was white, and the whites wouldn't want me because I acted black. It was okay for now, but if they sent me to Riker's Island, I was fucked. Maybe, literally. I was alone and alone at seventeen was no way to be on the Rock. Survival depended on alliances. There would be no alliances for me there.

At some point in time, my name was called. One of the cops escorted me through a maze of hallways into a cellblock of sorts. He tucked me into a solo cell with my very own wood slab bench and my very own shiny silver metal toilet. He went away for a while and then he came back and gave me a spam sandwich. That is where I waited for my turn on the bus to arraignment court. I was very happy to be out of the bullpen, but sleep eluded me. Thanks to God and the sick caseloads of the Bronx courts, I didn't go to Rikers Island that time. I must have been in that cell for about two days before I got my ticket. My court-appointed legal aid attorney asked the judge to give me an ACD because I was a first offender. That means 'adjourned in contemplation of dismissal.' The lawyer explained that if I stayed out of trouble for six months, my case would be dismissed. The prosecutor did not object and the deal was done. It took about three minutes.

Just like that, I was out. *'What a load of bullshit,'* I thought.

My father was plenty pissed about having to come up to the Bronx in a "Goddamned mother fucking taxi cab!" to pick up his pumpkin orange Mustang, and his son, but he got over it quick. He was just happy that I was okay. So was I. But when I got home, I was a celebrity. The white boy did his first bid. I forgot all about that scary shit I was thinking about in the bullpen. It was time to get back to the business of the street. All I had to do was to avoid getting locked up again. I would fail at that twice, but not within six months.

WASHING MACHINES

Most days we would hit four or five machines at a pop. The coin boxes were long and deep. If the timing was right, there would be a shitload of quarters in there.

I've been around this world a bit now, and I've seen some genuine poverty. Mexico, Peru, Thailand, and believe it or not, Tahiti. None of us were poor in that sense. Those people are dirt poor. We all had a roof and refrigerated food. Most families in the area were receiving some sort of public assistance, but no one was starving. On the other hand, there were protocols in the street. If you didn't dress right, you would be the subject of regular and fairly intense ridicule. You could suck it up, you could fight it out, or you could get your "threads" right. That meant you had to have a clean pair of jeans on every day, preferably pressed or with the creases sewn in. Wranglers were the standard. Lee or Levi was also acceptable. Sneakers had to have plenty of rubber on them and nothing less than converse or Pro-Keds would do. Adidas, Puma, and later on, Nike were top of the line. T-shirts had to be silk with matching boxers. Two pairs of sweat socks were worn with shorts in the summer. Don't ask me why, it was just what we did. The bottom pair were tube socks. The visible ones were usually calf-high wool with a two- or three-inch wide band of color around the top. No drooping! Sometimes you would need rubber bands to keep them up. In winter you had to have leather, a jacket that is. There were a few styles. Wrap coats came below the knee. They had a sash and no buttons, like a bathrobe. There were three quarter leather coats with Persian lamb collars, and belts buckled in the back like a vest. And there were Eisenhower leather jackets. These were waist-length two-tone jackets with an off-set zipper up the front and a leather belt around the bottom. There was a different dress code for parties or when you wanted to get 'clean.' A clean wardrobe consisted of a couple of double knit shirts or alpacas in the winter, some sharp slacks, maybe sharkskin, and at least one pair of Playboys. Playboys were shoes with a particular type of black crepe sole. The crepe was rubber, but not like a sneaker. It was black with a stippled texture. I remember there were real ones and fake ones. I couldn't tell you the difference and it didn't really matter. Either was acceptable. They could be found at Flagg Brothers and Regal Shoes. I can honestly say I never saw another white boy with a pair of those shoes on his feet, real or fake. I think I had three pairs.

We would go shopping some Sunday mornings down at Delancy and Orchard streets in the Bowery district of Manhattan. All the shops were century-old holes in the wall run by orthodox Jews. The rumor was that they had a superstition that if they made a sale to the first customer of the day, the rest of the day would be prosperous. So, we would get up early and try to be the first ones there. Then we would haggle or bargain on the price. But even if we got a bargain, we still needed money. And that kind of cash wasn't coming from home. We also needed money for food on the street, entertainment, and reefer, lots of reefer. So, we did whatever we could, wherever we were, and whenever an opportunity presented itself.

I recall strolling through Klein's department store one afternoon. Klein's had an entrance on Main Street and another on Roosevelt Avenue. So, it wasn't at all uncommon for us to cut through when going back and forth. I doubt that it saved any time, but it was an amusing and periodically profitable experience. On this particular day, it was just Kasseem and me heading somewhere. As we passed by one of the registers, I was watching the clerk counting out the customer's change. A cashier is not supposed to give the customer her change before closing the cash register drawer, but something told me that this particular clerk was about to break that rule. I slowed my pace and grabbed Kasseem by the shirttail. When he turned to me as if to say, 'What the fuck,' I gave him an up-nod toward the cashier. At that very moment, as if we all had rehearsed this episode, the cashier pivoted toward the customer to hand her the receipt and the change. Kasseem just reached over and with two fingers he snatched a stack of twenties right out of the open drawer. She closed her cash register and we just kept on keeping on. We were always vigilant for that kind of score. Always looking around. Always ready to strike in an instant. Of course, it's also that kind of focus that gets criminals busted. Anybody who doesn't worry about getting caught gets caught. We got away with that one.

Breaking into public washing machines and dryers was our number one source of income. We exercised far more care and preparation in that enterprise. There were coin-operated washers and dryers in the basement of just about every apartment building in the neighborhood. That was a lot of quarters there to be had. The first time I met this kid Kendu, he was trying to knock off a machine in my basement in the daytime. We bumped into this stranger when we got off the elevator and he needed to explain his presence. When Kasseem and I asked him what the fuck he was doing in my building, he started dancing around the question. I brushed by him into the laundry room and I saw the pry marks around the coin box. He had worked it about halfway out of the housing.

"Man! Look at all the quarters in there," I blurted to Kasseem.

All Kendu had was a little screwdriver and it was bent. Before we stumbled onto him, he was fishing out the quarters one by one. The box construction was initially simple. There was a drawer about five-inches wide and eight-inches deep that slid into the coin mechanism housing. Once in place, the key could be turned and metal flaps inside the box would slide up behind a lip on the housing, locking the drawer in place. The metal was soft, but Kendu's little pocket screwdriver really couldn't get the job done. Now Kendu, by rights, should have gotten a beating for stinging my building but the sight of all those quarters put a whole different spin on the situation. I owned a monster screwdriver that some fireman dropped the last time a tenant set the garbage incinerator chute on fire. All the apartment buildings used to burn their garbage. There was a chute on every floor where the occupants would drop the trash down to the basement. In the basement was an incinerator like a mini crematorium. The garbage would be slowly burned and reduced to ash. The ash was then shoveled into metal pails and left outside for the New York City Department of Sanitation to remove. The cans were incredibly heavy. The system worked well for its time. Of course, it created massive air pollution. The other problem was that when the superintendent took a few days off, the trash piled up in the chute. If people couldn't put their garbage in, they would just leave it on the floor by the chute. In no time, the word would get out to the roach and vermin communities and you can guess the rest. So inevitably someone would go in and set the trash in the chute on fire. Unfortunately, the incineration system only worked with a controlled burn starting at the bottom. When someone ignited the garbage on the fourth floor somewhere, the result would be a veritable inferno and a smoke-choked apartment building.

I went upstairs to get my mammoth fireman screwdriver and, in less than two hours, we had successfully emptied the coins from the two washers and two dryers in that laundry room. With so much change in our pockets, we could hardly keep our pants up. We introduced Kendu to the other kids and explained the big caper.

"All you have to do is keep working around the edges and out she comes."

Kendu came from about five blocks away on Colden Street near Booth Memorial Hospital. He didn't want to hit the machines near his apartment, so he came down by ours. We decided to let him hang with us, but the next day we got a couple more screwdrivers and we wiped out his building first.

From there, the town was wide open. Most of us got pretty good at it and could do a machine in about ten minutes. We would take turns at looking out or 'laying chicky' and nobody ever got caught as we moved from building to building and block to block.

There *was* this one kid, a junky from Corona. He was working on his own. In our hunt for new targets, we came across a few machines that had already been jacked. You didn't have to be a scholar to put that caper together. He came to the wrong neighborhood. We spotted him one night going into the basement of one of our buildings on Parsons Boulevard. Little Carlos sprinted to a payphone about two blocks away and called 911. Then we just sat back and watched the action. We set that boy up for a takedown. The cops busted him in the act. They thought they caught a one-man crime wave. He never found out what we did. Nobody was allowed to mess with our money.

Most days we would hit four or five machines at a pop. The coin boxes were long and deep. If we hit it right, there would be a shitload of quarters in there. The trick was to get there shortly before the guy from the company came to collect. Through trial and error, we were able to estimate the collection schedule. And if there were only a few quarters in one of the machines, we would walk away from the whole bank knowing that the others would be equally lean. If the first one was shy, they all would be. No sense in wasting a lot of time for a couple of dollars. We would wait a few days for the boxes to fill up. Then we would go back and finish the job.

Discreetly moving that many coins from one place to another presented another serious logistical dilemma. The first couple of times, we just filled our pockets. When we came swaggering down the street with our Wranglers busting out the sides, people noticed. We definitely didn't want to be noticed. There were other problems too. Once our pants were full, we were done for the day. We might be onto the mother lode and have to quit early. Or worse, we might have to leave some cash behind. But the biggest danger of all was a confrontation. I knew that five pounds of coins would really slow me down if I had to run, and I figured I would be like a human slot machine just spitting out quarters all the way and leaving a trail to follow. Clearly, it was essential that we came up with another method of carrying the goods. Enter the laundry soapbox.

There were always multiple empty cardboard laundry detergent boxes in the garbage can of every laundry room. Pouring the coins into the box and walking out carrying a clothing soap carton was a lot less conspicuous than bulging pockets. Not only that, but it gave us camouflage. Walking out of a laundry room with a soapbox looked right. We also took to carrying our tools in another box. What a great cover! This little activity kept us fat for a long time. Meanwhile, Coinmach was losing big money and they weren't taking it well. Coinmach was the company that did the collections and the maintenance of the machines. They weren't taking these losses lying down. Unbeknownst to us, they were developing a new pry-proof box that just appeared one day all over town. And it worked. They had installed a big fat metal plate on the front of the box and a hood that stuck straight out about four inches. That made it impossible to wedge a pry bar behind the plate. The days of using a screwdriver to jimmy those machines had come to an end. Pretty smart. And so began our chess game with the good people of Coinmach.

Undaunted, we decided to try an electric drill. We did experience some limited success. The keyholes on the box were made for those round kinds of keys with the notches all around and one little nipple on top. If you trained the drill bit dead center of that round keyhole, eventually it would penetrate the metal and the lock would turn and open. But there were many drawbacks.

The drills were big and heavy and they had to be plugged in. We found ourselves having to carry an extension cord too. That was too much gear.

Another problem was that drills were machines and machines are noisy. The screwdrivers weren't silent but they were quiet. Drills were far more likely to draw the attention of a tenant dining or trying to sleep in the rooms above. The bits weren't that great either. There was no such thing as titanium back then. There were bits made for metal, but what did we know about that? We stole the drills from local construction sites and contractors vehicles. Whatever bits were in the box with the drill were the bits we would use. Most of them were probably wood bits. It took a very long, very loud time to bore through the lock and the bit usually got stuck. Once you got it in a certain depth, it probably wasn't coming out. I learned that the hard way. I got my hand crushed one afternoon when the bit jammed and the drill spun around and pinned my knuckles between the trigger and that security shroud Coinmach installed on the machine to keep us from prying it. One of the other boys was on 'chicky' when the elevator passed the first floor and was still coming down. The 'chicky' gave me the high sign and we both bailed out. My hand was all bloody and in pain. The bit had burrowed too deeply and I couldn't get it out. I had to leave the whole drill protruding prominently from the lock just south of the cover. The plan was to go back for it later.

The laundry room had little rectangular windows that were up high at the top of the wall that looked outside at the ground level. Snugged up against a parked car outside, my partner and I were able to monitor the laundry lady through one of the windows. It appeared as if she hadn't even noticed the drill. Once she got her clothing churning, she headed back upstairs and we went back to work. We had to hurry because she might have noticed after all, and she might be calling the cops from her apartment. I was able to finish the job. I had to leave the bit in the lock when I tossed the drawer in the garbage, but that shit happened from time to time.

Obviously, drills were not the way to go. Now, we needed another way to get into those machines. One afternoon a Coinmach mechanic left a ring of keys on the seat of his car in the summer. He left his windows open and this kid named CB snatched them. CB was a friend of Kendu, also from Colden Street.

He fit into our crew just fine. We split the keys up and spent the next few days walking all over town trying them out. Only a handful wound up working. Of course, we kept using them over and over, returning to the same machines every other week. They reaped some easy coin for a while until the locks were changed. We needed a new angle on this thing. I can't tell you who came up with the idea of burning the plates off the front of the coin boxes, or how he even knew how to do it. It was probably Thumper. He had instincts about things of that kind.

The torch was composed of two parts. There was a long brass tube with a threaded female valve on one end and a nozzle on the other. The valve screwed onto a bottle of propane. It came boxed with a flint lighter. You had to squeeze the lighter so that a sharp piece on one side scraped against a round flint on the other and created a spark. The first step was to turn on the valve on the propane bottle to allow the gas out, then hold the flint to the side of the gas stream emitted from the nozzle, and make the spark. The spark would ignite the gas and then you could control the flame pattern from wide to narrow by using the valve like a water hose. Clearly, it was extremely dangerous especially in the hands of some stoned out teenaged gangsters working inside basement laundry rooms at night. I literally tremble when I think about all of the injuries and destruction we could have caused with those things both to ourselves and to the people living in those old tenement buildings. Kids, especially boys, just don't think about shit like that. But the torch did prove to be highly effective, very fast, and almost silent. That device vaulted us into a new realm of coin box criminality. It took some experimentation with flame placement, but the protective plates began melting right off. Then, it was simply a matter of jiggling the box so that the lock plates would fall down.

One lesson was hard learned for one of the boys. I don't remember who it was who tried to snatch the first scalding hot coin box out of a machine.

When you melt the face off the plate metal, everything around it gets hot, including the coins. After those first few burnt fingers, it became clear that the box could not be handled manually. Every laundry room had a slop sink for the washing machines to drain into. The box had to be lifted out with a screwdriver and placed in the slop sink for a cold shower. The box would sizzle and steam would rise, but wet coins were still United States currency, and we collected bushels of them. Of course, the torches were a little bulky, but they fit into the larger laundry detergent boxes in the garbage pails. I guess you could say we 'cleaned-up' on the laundry machines. Today the NYPD would have a burglary task force on the case. Dopes like us would be busted in no time. But not back then!

After about a year of getting burnt, Coinmach came up with a counter move. It was a burn-proof plate. This time they had 'The Family' in check, but we had one more play. Not quite a checkmate yet. By then, I had my driver's license, and I was driving my parents' car, a 1969 Mustang. My mother didn't drive anymore because of her 'condition' and my father preferred to walk most of the time. It was hard to find parking around our block and we would sometimes have to leave the car several blocks from home. Wherever the old man was going was usually closer than where he parked, and if the car was close, he wouldn't want to give up the good spot. So, once I passed my road test, the boys and I were on the road almost all the time. This, of course, created a new expense, gas money.

On one stunningly pleasant spring afternoon, a couple of us were sitting in the Mustang outside my building out on Sanford Avenue. We were listening to WBLS on the AM dial, when we spotted the Coinmach man emerging from the basement with one sack of quarters in each hand. He had a light-colored Chevy, double parked on the street with no logo or sign on it. There was no way to tell it was a Coinmach car except that the guy had the uniform shirt on. He put the bags in the trunk, got in, and drove away.

"Did you see that shit?"

"Fuck yeah! Let's see where the motherfucker goes."

We followed.

He led us to about ten different buildings until he took off down Northern Boulevard with an air of 'I'm done for the day.' Perhaps a Robert DeNiro character would have followed the bag man back to the Coinmach coin depot, to get a handle on all the other bag men that were surely coming into the barn at about the same time, each bursting with quarters. The Hollywood gangster character would have then staked the place out in the mornings over the next few days to trace the different pickup routes and plan a Lufthansa style heist. The boys in the family were no DeNiros. We were small-time hoods living moment to moment as much for the thrill as for the reward. Still, this was going to be a big caper for us. We would focus just on one route and one guy. Our dilemma? Should we break into the trunk or just intimidate the guy and take the whole car? Robbery wasn't our forte, apart from the occasional drug dealer. Kasseem did some diner stickups with a couple of other junkies back when he was strung out on heroin, but most of us preferred to avoid confrontation when we were working. Either choice, robbery, or break in, we would be working in daylight.

The next week on the same day, I had the Mustang parked outside the last place the bag man picked up from the day we tailed him. It was a building on Northern Boulevard near Bowne Street. I was doing surveillance work and I didn't even know it. If he traveled the same route every time, his trunk would be filled with coins by the time he arrived. Like the hands on my Timex, Mr. Coinmach showed up and emptied the machines. He was inside for about eight minutes. He went in through the lobby and came out of the basement door. The superintendent probably buzzed him in or maybe he had a key because we found the lobby door locked. I could always get someone to open the door. My routine was to push some buttons on the top floors. When the inquiring voice came over the intercom, I would put on a Spanish accent and say, "I lews de key please." The buzzer blared, the lock released, and in I would go. I wanted to scope the place out, so I pulled my scam and got buzzed in. The elevator took me to the basement and the laundry room wasn't hard to find. When the dryers were going, the aroma from the exhaust filled the halls. I literally sniffed them out. There were two dryers and two washers in that room. Interestingly, they had the old coin boxes without the pry plates; the kind you could crack with a screwdriver. We had never come up that far north in the neighborhood. No matter, we were on to bigger and better things now. I had Carlos with me. He pretended to open, dump, and close each box. He was trying to figure out how much time the Coinmach guy would spend in the basement so we would know how fast we would have to work.

"How long did that take?" he asked.

"How the fuck do I know?"

That was actually a pretty good idea, but we hadn't discussed it beforehand, I didn't time it and now someone was coming.

"Let's go."

I had already approximated that he was down there for about eight minutes when I watched him come and go. Back in the car, the decision was made. It was going to be a break in. Robazz had expressed interest in getting involved and he would be a good choice. He was a solid dude with big balls, and he'd never rat anybody out. He also had experience stealing cars by slapping out the ignitions and starting them with a screwdriver. A slapper or a pulley was a cumbersome steel rod used by body shops to pull out dents. In its auto theft adaptation, it was screwed into the ignition lock and a sliding weight was slammed down the shaft, against the handle, away from the steering column. The force of the impact would yank out the entire lock system, and the car could then be started with a screwdriver. If a crook was good, he could yank the ignition with two or three slaps. Robazz had the tools and the experience. He was our guy.

This would be a ballsy play. Robazz told us that stealing the whole car was not the best option. "Sometimes them ignition locks get stubborn. It might take too long. We got a better shot at slappin out the trunk lock. That shit's a lot weaker."

So, three kids were going to bust open a car trunk on a busy mid-day on Northern Boulevard street, make off with umpteen sacks of quarters, and load them into an orange mustang legally registered to R. Semmes Lowry. I said it was ballsy, not smart.

The caper was actually planned pretty well. We waited a couple of weeks and caught a rainy day. There would be a lot fewer people on the street in the rain. On the job, guys would say, "Rain is the best policeman." Even the bad guys stay inside. Not that day. Not us.

Carlos went ahead on foot and planted a supermarket shopping cart on the sidewalk near the place where the bag man parked the last time. There was a fire hydrant very close to the entrance to the building. That's where Coinmach left the Chevy both times we saw him. Carlos left a sheet in the wagon to cover the cash. Robazz and I took position in the Mustang where we could see Coinmach when he arrived. Carlos joined us in the car. He was getting my seats wet from the rain and I was pissed.

"Why didn't you bring a fucking umbrella?"

"Fuck off! *Maricon!*" (faggot in Spanish).

We wouldn't have much time. Carlos would be on chicky. Robazz would grab the wagon and slap out the trunk lock while I parked the car around the corner. I would run back and help Robazz empty the trunk. When Carlos saw the guy coming out of the basement, his job was to look up at a window and yell, "Bobbayy, Yo Bobbayyy" like he was calling for a friend to come out. That would be our signal to close the trunk and split with the bread. It was important to close the trunk. Most likely Mr. Coinmach wouldn't be carrying a screwdriver so he wouldn't be able to re-open the trunk. With a little luck, he might not report the theft until he got back to the coin depot and actually found the money missing.

When Coinmach arrived, my hands were shaking. He parked on the fire hydrant near the corner of the block and Carlos hopped out. I slid off the curb before Robazz jumped out to give the guy time to get to the door. As I twisted the Mustang around the corner, I could see my man slapping at the lock in my rearview mirror. Things were going well. My pulse was racing as I grabbed a spot about halfway down the side street. By the time I reached Robazz, he was already filling the wagon. As the last bag came out, he said, "Get the trunk Kev." I slammed it shut.

Turning quickly, I saw the sheet flapping outside the cart. Robazz wasn't running, but he was moving fast. I caught up at the corner. As I yanked up the sheet to cover the loot and the tools, one of the bags spilled and we started leaving a trail of quarters. Just for an instant, I thought about Hansel and Gretel. That thought was broken by the sound of "Bobbeyyy, Bobbeyyy." Carlos told us later that he stopped the bag man and asked him if he knew where the public library was, just to slow him down a little. Pretty shrewd play. The guy gave him careful directions while we loaded my trunk. Carlos then set off to find his 'book,' and Robazz, and I were on the road before Coinmach knew he'd been hit. Back in the carriage room, down in my basement, we divvied up the prize; twenty-six sacks of roughly $200 bucks each. The total was about five grand! That was huge for us. The three of us did some heavy spending for the next few weeks. Literally!

Typical apartment house laundry room/cash cow.

Kasseem and me counting money from some "big score."

TAKIN' A TRIP

What's closer to New York, Jamaica, or Hawaii?

The kid's family name was Pinkney. He lived in Astoria and he worshipped Thumper. I have no clue how they met, but the day Thumper brought him around the neighborhood was the day Mr. Pinkney got his street name. Thumper introduced the guy to us as a group, "This is Phil Pinkney." He could have just said "Phil," but he said "Phil Pinkney." That was all it took. Ballah just blurted it out.

"Pigmy? This fuckin guy is Pigmy? Yo fellas, meet Pigmy," and off it went.

"Yo Pigmy!"

"Wassup Pigmy?"

"Pig Meeeeeeeeeee!"

And on and on. The boys were crying with hilarity. And you know what? Good old Pigmy sucked it up and took it like a champ. He was chiseled like granite with super light skin, deep orange freckles, and reddish hair. He had a most unique appearance, indeed. He stood out almost as much as I did. Pigmy was a rock-solid five foot eight, but nobody fucked with him, ever. I can't remember him ever getting mad at anyone, let alone getting into a fight.

In my recollection, Pigmy never hurt another person, but there was no doubt that he could have. He was "farm boy" powerful, with the sweetest temperament out of all of the kids I knew. If Pigmy had been a dog, his name would have been Blue. It was one of those inexplicable phenomena. We always ranked on him; sometimes mercilessly, but somehow, we all just knew not to ever put our hands on the guy. No one would have anyway because everybody loved him! Sometimes, he would entertain us by doing a series of backflips and handstands. He was agile and acrobatic.

Pigmy was a burglar. That's all he did. He didn't do robberies and he didn't sell drugs, but he loved breaking into buildings. He was also an amazing climber. That is a skill that comes in mighty handy for a burglar because sometimes the shit you want is not on the ground floor.

I was laying chicky on a caper for him and Ballah one night. It was some kind of factory or warehouse that backed up to a thirty-some, odd foot chain-link fence between the warehouse and the Long Island Railroad tracks on the opposite side of the Bland Housing Project. Inside the building, the boys tripped the burglar alarm system. There was nothing I could do now but watch the show. As the cops closed in, Pigmy and Ballah came flying out the same second-floor window they had gone in. But instead of coming down, Ballah got on Pigmy's back, and Pigmy carried him all the way up as he scaled that big-ass fence to the safety of the railroad platform, high above that second-story window. From there, they just took off down the tracks. I got out of there too, of course. That was one amazing feat of strength.

One particular Sunday afternoon, I was sitting in the Mustang waiting for someone outside the B wing. Pigmy came up on me and jumped into the passenger side.

"Yo Kev, check this out."

He opened up this satchel he was carrying and it was stuffed full of cash.

"Woaaa! How much you got there?" I blurted.

"A little over three thousand dollahs!" he boasted. "C'mon, take me over to the electronics shop, I wanna buy me a stereo."

I completely forgot about who I was waiting for and sped off to Prince Street to the stereo store down by the Projects. I pulled into the loading zone and Pigmy hopped out and ran in. He was back in no time with a huge boxed stereo set. We had to tie it into the trunk. I agreed to drive him home to Astoria to drop it off.

"Yo, Kevin man, you know what we should do?" He didn't wait for an answer. "We should take a trip."

"Whadda ya mean, like a road trip? Drive somewhere?"

"Nah man, I'm talkin about like flyin out to Hawaii or Jamaica. Somethin like that. Ya know what I'm sayin?"

I was sixteen and he was fifteen. I wasn't passing this up.

"Fuckin 'A' man, I'm down with that shit."

"So how do we do it? I wanna leave tomorrow."

"Well, afta we drop off the stereo, we'll just drive over to the airport and set it up."

"Cool man, let's do that. But I don't wanna be flyin too long. What's closer, Jamaica or Hawaii?"

"I don't know man." And I didn't. "We can find out when we get there."

JFK was not nearly as crazy as it is now and parking was easy. John F. Kennedy airport used to be called Idlewild airport. After President Kennedy was shot, they changed the name. We walked up to one of the ticket counters. It could have been Pan Am or TWA. I asked the lady behind the counter, "What's closer to fly to? Jamaica or Hawaii?"

She and her coworker could not hide their amusement at this naïve question. I instantly realized that the two must be very far apart. We booked two round trip tickets to Montego Bay, leaving the next day for three nights. Pigmy peeled off the cash, and the lady gave us the tickets. When we asked the lady about a hotel, she pointed us to a wall of phones with hotel names above each. I picked up the Holiday Inn hotline and called us in a reservation.

With that, we left the airport. I told my parents the truth about what happened and they didn't flinch. They really had no clue how to handle my situation, and they were so wrapped up in their own shit that they kind of threw up their hands. That night, with the crew, it was a different story.

"Where y'all niggahs been all fuckin day?" Tookie demanded.

Pigmy had bought everybody some wine and reefer before we went back. He passed out the goodies and told them the story. He went into detail about how he pulled an air conditioner unit out of the back wall of the carpet dealer on Main Street the night before. He was by himself. There were only a few bucks in the cash register, so he started rummaging around in the office. There was an alarm system, but it looked like it was only on the doors and windows. Pigmy had come in through the hole in the wall where the air-conditioner used to be. He said he was hoping he might find a gun in a desk drawer, but he came up empty. Just as he was getting ready to leave, a second peak under a desk revealed the satchel. The cash was in a couple of night deposit drop bags.

Before they had ATMs, some banks had night deposit drop boxes. If a commercial depositor had an account there, the bank would issue him a key to the box and a few leather pouches with locking zippers. The business owner would fill the bags with the day's receipts, lock the zippers, and bring them to the bank. He would have to unlock the box on the wall outside the building, drop in the bags, and lock it up again. Why this guy hadn't made the drop is unknown. Pigmy cut the cash out of the bags before he bumped into me. The rest, you already know.

"Hole Lee Shit!" The gang first reacted with jubilation and amazement. That quickly changed to jealousy, and then descended into resentment directed primarily in my direction.

"Why the fuck didn't you take me?"

"I want to go too."

"Why you takin this muthah fuckah?"

Pigmy was starting to get nervous. He was feeling the pressure. "Yo man, he got a car and he knows how to get shit done. That's it. Don't mean nuthin."

Tookie got right in my face over it. "Yo man, I think you took advantage of my man Pigmy."

"Look man, Pigmy came to me for a ride. I took care of him and the trip was his fuckin idea, so back up off me. Ain't that right Pigmy?"

"Yeah Took, that's the way it went down. Just like that." Pigmy's tone changed a bit. He didn't want anybody to be pissed at him, but he definitely didn't want people to think he let me take advantage of him. That would have hurt his street cred. And the truth is that I didn't take advantage of him and that was exactly the way it went down. Opportunity knocked, I answered, and the next day we flew down to the right side of Montego Bay.

TAKE-OFFS

It all made perfect sense. Take a loaded gun to a marijuana rip-off with a baby in the back seat.

I never robbed anybody, but I used to 'take people off for their shit.' I bought drugs, sold drugs, and stole drugs. The brothers and I knew every small-time dealer within a few miles. Crocheron Park, Alley Pond Park, and all of the public schoolyards were the outdoor markets. And a periodic trip to the Bronx wasn't out of the question now that we had the Mustang. Some dealers were bad assed dudes and not to be fucked with. Others were just kids 'playing a game' to support their own taste for the stuff and to feel the rush. There were pushers out there who didn't even need the money. Their parents had plenty. They were just in it for the jazz. The trick was to know who was who. Who would be the easy mark?

There was this security guard hired one summer, by one of the apartment buildings, down by Colden Street to watch over the place at night. He had an office in the basement and mostly he was bored all night. So, he started selling nickel bags of reefer. This somewhat infringed on our periodic business, but he didn't have many customers because he didn't want to jeopardize his job.

He also befriended 'The Family' and turned us all on every night. He was paying the tax.

Maybe he was naive or maybe he got careless from the smoke, but the guard let one of the boys into the office one night to roll a joint, and he tipped his hand as to where he kept his stash. That was that, while we were all outside partying with him, Ballah slid in through the window and snatched the reefer. It was about a half pound. Vengeance was not an option because he couldn't know for sure that we set it up. We were all there smoking his shit when it went down. But that was the last time he got high with us. Nobody gave a shit about anybody else. Just get yours at any cost. Trick people, befriend them, and then turn on them, or just beat their ass and take what you want. We swore we would never do that to each other, but there were times that we did …

We weren't racist about where the money came from. It was always clear to me that the black kids would prefer to steal from white kids, but in the end, given the choice, my guys would take anybody off. However, in this game, it was mostly whites that we targeted. One reason was that they were outside of our neighborhood. It was okay to steal from local people behind their backs, but straight up taking their shit out of their hands was not good business. Every day, your victim would see you, and sooner or later, he might seek revenge. The other reason the white kids were better targets for drug take offs was that they were usually the ones in it for fun. I mean, you're not going to go after a biker, but some preppy boy from Whitestone? No contest. And if you take a guy's drugs, he's not going to tell anyone; not the police and probably not his father. He might have some friends, but we had friends too.

There was one more thing that set the white guys apart. That was the variety of drugs they had available. In our neck of the concrete, it was mostly reefer and coke. Occasionally, some hashish came around. The preppy kids had stuff like mescaline, opium, and my favorite, THC. THC was a pill that was supposed to be concentrated cannabis. God knows what it really was. I don't even like to think about it, but the 'honkies' had it sometimes, and it was a break from the norm with a five-hour buzz.

So, one summer afternoon, a couple of us went cruising a few spots on a THC quest. Two guys we knew through previous deals were standing on a corner outside a local public school playground, on a bus stop, somewhere on the north-east end of the 109 Precinct. One had a shopping bag in his hand. I pushed the nose of the Mustang into the curb. I had no air conditioning so the window was already open. Kasseem was riding shotgun and he asked the kids if anybody had any THC. The one with the bag said, "No, but check this out" and he lifted the paper bag and plopped it in Kasseem's lap. "I'm looking to do it by the ounce. It's primo shit," he said. With that, from inside the sack, my partner lifts a very plump plastic bag, sticks his face in, and takes a slow deep inhale. As his face began to turn in my direction, the light turned green. I dropped the tranny into drive and just pulled away. I got a glimpse of the boys in the rearview mirror, and they were stunned. They were just standing in the middle of the street, watching the Mustang getting smaller. They must have discussed the wishful possibility that we were just messing with them, but that had to pass quickly. The haul was close to a pound. We suspected they might come looking for us because they knew where we could be found. But they never showed.

After those scores, we were hooked on drug dealers. Most went pretty easy because we did our homework. The routine was a three-man job. I was always the driver. Today, I cannot imagine my stupidity. I was driving my father's bright pumpkin Mustang. There was only one car in New York City like that. You could spot it anywhere. The car wasn't always pumpkin colored. It was originally beige. The old man let me start driving it when I got my junior license at the age of sixteen. I started banging into things forthwith. I had my first accident three days after I got my license. One particular accident, however, was super bad. There were three of us in the car and we all could have died that night on the Brooklyn Queens Expressway. There's no telling where we were coming from, I just don't remember. All I know is that we were coming home from Brooklyn and we had just crossed the Kosciuszko Bridge. The car was in the center lane and we were all blitzed. Jose had shotgun, and I think this guy we called Moon Mullins was in the back. He went on to become a New York State Trooper. We never thought twice about driving stoned. Every day we were stoned and every day we drove. Well, on this particular night, with WWRL blasting on the AM radio, Jose yelled at me that I was passing our exit. We were supposed to get off on the Long Island Expressway East. No sweat boys, I'll just stop the car here in the center lane and back up. CAN YOU IMAGINE!! Never underestimate the stupidity of a stoned-out sixteen-year-old boy, behind the wheel of his father's Mustang, with WWRL or any other thing roaring over the car's sound system.

There I went backing up in the center lane of the Brooklyn Queens Expressway. In no time divided by two, our car got blasted by a great big four-door Chevy Impala. That guy, then, got creamed by a compact from Connecticut. Jose saw it coming. He just kept saying, "Yo, Kevin man. Yo, Kevin man!" and BOOM! The back of his seat broke right off and he fell in Moon's lap. It was a miracle the car didn't blow up. The gas tank was literally crushed. The body mechanic said that the only thing that saved us was a full tank of gas.

"If that tank hadda bin filled with fumes insteada gas, them boys wudda bin day-ed."

The car was totaled, but the old man had it repaired and painted. He must have gotten a hell of a deal because that paint was definitely some color that somebody else didn't want. And that's how the Mustang got to be pumpkin orange.

Anyway, when it came to stinging, I was always the driver, shotgun would be the strong arm, and one guy would ride in the back for extra muscle. The dealer would be lured to the car for a pre-arranged meeting. Most would be reluctant to put the dope in the car. The strong arm and the muscle had to get out and flash some cash. Once one of my guys had the stuff in hand, he would toss it in the car, and I'd throw it in the back seat. By then, the dealer was usually terrified and would walk or run away. If the dealer had someone with him, one of the boys would sometimes pull a knife or just punch one of them square in the face. From there, it was simply a matter of getting back in the car and driving away.

It didn't always go silky smooth. Sometimes, we had to divert from the plan. That was usually a problem. There was a kid in Bayside selling ounces of marijuana. Robazz set him up for a quarter-pound deal. I didn't know the guy, I just knew the time and place. It felt from the beginning that we should have called it off, but arrogance and a general feeling of invincibility took over. The deal was going down in the daytime at some garden apartments around 192nd Street by the Long Island Rail Road tracks. The guy wanted to do it inside his apartment, and the boys wanted me to come in with them thinking another white face might relax him. This was not our M.O. Who knows what the fuck he might have had in there! I did not like it. When we got there, there was no place to park. I suggested I sit in the car.

"C'mon man. Suppose he's got people in there? We need you inside man," was the response I got. I didn't want to walk out that door with a quarter pound of pot to find some cops writing me a parking ticket. The car had to be parked on the other side of the elevated railroad tracks, and we walked back.

'Bad. This is not good,' I thought.

There was a bunch of local kids hanging out on the stoops and in the streets, drinking beer and some of them had that 'What the fuck are you doing here?' look.

"I don't like this," I said.

"Just be cool man" is what came back. I was cool. We went up the stairs and knocked. The door opened and the guy let us in. He didn't look too tough and I relaxed a little. We were in the living room and I could see the kitchen.

We want to keep him out of there, I thought, Too many knives and shit.

I asked to use the toilet so I could get a peek at the bedroom. Unfortunately, the bedroom door was closed. I didn't want to really pee. If the shit hit the fan suddenly, I might be running out of there with my dick in my hand. I just stood there for a minute and listened as the guy asked to see the money. LeLe was a very big, very intimidating guy, who ran with us from time to time, and we had him there that day. He was carrying the flash cash. This was the same guy who would be shot and crippled by Ballah years later. LeLe was short for Leslie.

"Now let me see the shit," I heard.

Time to get back to the living room.

I passed the guy in the hall. He walked into the bedroom and closed the door, but I did get a glimpse inside before the door slammed shut and I didn't notice anyone else. When he stepped back into the living room, our boy was carrying four baggies, presumably one ounce each. He handed two to me and two to Robazz as he put out his hand to LeLe and asked why we needed three guys to cop four ounces of grass.

"Because we ain't payin you asshole," LeLe replied as he put the money back in his pocket.

"Mother fucker! Mother fucker!"

We were already out the door.

When we reached the bottom of the stoop there came a screaming voice, "Yo, these niggers just robbed me. They robbed me, man."

The beer drinkers instantly sprang into action. They just morphed into a posse. We lit out running with them in close pursuit. I went one way, and Robazz and LeLe went the other. It worked out that the local boys were more interested in tasting black blood than mine because most of them went after the brothers.

Not knowing my way around that area, it took me about five blocks and more than a few back yards to shake my tail, but I shook them. The problem was that I still had to get to my car, which was right back there where it all started. I wandered around a while until dusk, and then I had an idea. I hopped a fence and climbed the dirt berm up to the railroad tracks. As I made my way along the tracks in the fading light, I kept a vigilant eye on the business below while keeping a comfortable distance between me and the electrified third rail. It wasn't long before my eyes came upon the posse regrouped below. There were beer-swilling Baysidians everywhere. This drug dealer's robbery had sparked a spontaneous block party. No doubt they were all talking about how it would have gone if, "Those niggers tried to do that shit to me."

The thrill of it was that they were all looking for me, while I was perched high above watching every one of them. I could dash and stop at will as long as I stayed low. I was able to track every move they made. Sure, I was somewhat exposed, but the possibility of being spotted gave me a charge. When I reached the spot above where my car was parked, I could proceed at my leisure. With my expanded peripheral vision, I needn't approach my vehicle until the proverbial coast was crystal clear.

Fast forward about a decade. Police officer Kevin Lowry was operating Nassau County Police car 420, in Oceanside New York, in a snowstorm in January of 1985. A call came out at about 0200 hours or 2 a.m., "Robbery just occurred at the 7/11 store on Lawson Boulevard in Oceanside. Four male whites, one armed with a knife, threatened the clerk with death. Made off with an unknown amount of US currency. Last seen northbound on Lawson Blvd. in a light colored four door sedan. Unknown make, model, or plate number."

Guess what? Besides police cruisers, the only vehicle on the road that night in the blizzard was the stick-up crew's car. They were stupider than I used to be. Probably strung out.

They *won't get far,* I surmised as I started a slow ride in the general direction of 7/11.

"No sense in getting there in a hurry, the bad guys are already gone," I thought out loud. I planned to pull over anything that was moving.

It was no surprise that they were stopped by car 405 operated by PO Jack Sullivan in East Rockaway about three minutes later. That was his regular car post. Jack was able to latch onto three of the four perpetrators. The fourth dude took off on foot and got away. Needless to say, every car in the Fourth precinct that night was available to assist in the search of the escaped desperado. Just about every car on the East end responded to the area. Their operators all jumped out, fanned out, and began searching for the elusive number four. All of them, that is, except Officer Lowry in car 420. I had been transported back in my mind to circa 1975 when I myself had been the subject of such a manhunt.

He sees them, I thought, *But they don't see him. If he can make it to the railroad tracks, he's home free.*

While twenty some-odd cops were clambering around in the snow, in the dark; I tucked my cruiser in among some trucks parked in a lot by the train crossing on Atlantic Avenue, turned up the heat, lit a cigar, and waited for my boy to come to me. It took about an hour and a half before I saw the lone chilly figure lumbering down the tracks.

"420 to headquarters. I'm southbound on the railroad tracks from the East Rockaway station in pursuit of one suspect from the 7/11 robbery. Advise the railroad to suspend service."

I wasn't about to get my feet wet. I drove that Dodge Diplomat right down the tracks after that character! The guy bolted through a gap in the fence, and I tried to squeeze the Dodge into the same hole. I slipped into the slot and got hung up on a huge railroad tie lurking beneath the thin layer of freshly fallen powder. The front tires bounced over but the car hung up like a see-saw. The gas pedal was impotent and the thief was getting away. "420 in foot pursuit of the subject, south on Lawson Boulevard. Request assistance." The fucking guy got the jump on me, and I lost him.

Maybe driving down the tracks wasn't such a good idea after all, I thought. It allowed the guy to take evasive action.

Suddenly, I spotted his footprints in the snow. Now, I was reinvigorated.

I'm gonna bag this guy, I heard myself think. So, I started tracking those footprints in the fresh damp snow like Daniel Boone in the woods. By now,

I was joined by Andre Amin and Phil Blessinger. They were working in plain clothes that day. I stood at the back door of their unmarked car and we zipped along, chasing the sneaker tracks. The footprints came to an abrupt dead-end at a padlocked garage door at the end of a residential driveway.

"Who's this guy, Houdini?" Phil questioned.

It took a few seconds before I put it together.

"He's on the roof!" I blurted. "Hey, it's over buddy. C'mon down."

Phil and Andre had instinctively taken up positions at opposing corners of the garage so the bad guy couldn't escape. They were a couple of pros, and it was a privilege to work with them.

His head popped up first. Looking side to side, he assessed his predicament. With guns pointed at him from three directions, he raised his hands and slowly rose to his feet. Phil and Andre clambered to the roof while I continued to talk to the guy.

"Just take it easy man and nobody gets hurt. It's just a bullshit robbery, don't make it worse."

Andre cuffed the guy and along with Phil, he literally slid him off the roof to the waiting hand of the three other cops who had arrived on the scene.

"Good grab, Spike," said my buddy Benzenberg.

"Yeah, way to go man," was the general response from the rest of the team.

My youth on the streets of New York City had a direct impact on my success as a police officer on Long Island, and my ability to survive with minimal injury. I knew what the bad guys were going to do because I knew what I did. I always called on my experiences and it paid off many times over.

Back on the tracks, I saw that the Bayside crew had gotten bored and broke up. I slid down the hill and hopped in my ride. Thankfully, it started right up, and I was on my way home. I still had the two ounces of pot in my pocket. When I reunited with the fellas, my story, of course, was that I lost the dope in the melee. Funny coincidence, the other guys lost theirs too. Never trust a crook. That particular event had a happy ending, at least for me. There were others that could have irreversibly changed my life and, even now, I shudder when I think about them.

The robbery took place in the top floor apartment on the right.
The stoops were full of tough white kids swilling beer and ready to rumble.

Kasseem set up a dealer one night. He told me about the job a few days in advance. The guy would broker the purchase of a pound of reefer for us. It wasn't his shit. He would be doing a favor for Kasseem and probably getting a finder's fee. The bigger dealer would never show his face. The job would go down around the corner from the big dealer's house. Our little dealer, the target, was supposed to have the product in the street and we were supposed to pay him. Kasseem said the kid wasn't any kind of threat, just a local pothead and nickel bag dealer. A real pushover. So easy that Kasseem and I were going to do the job alone.

We had it all planned when out of the blue, like an episode of the *Little Rascals*, Kasseem's mother told him he had to watch his nephew while she went to work.

"But Mom, we got this big thing planned. We're gonna take off a drug dealer."

He didn't say that, but that's what we were thinking. The deal was set. We had some flash money and the planets were all aligned. No turning back. What could we do?

She said, "I don't care what y'all doin. You gotta watch Joe."

When Ms. Marlene made up her mind, there was no changing it.

First things first, we needed someone to watch the kid. Joe was all of about eighteen months old. I enlisted the assistance of CB. I told CB we were just going to cop some reefer. I didn't tell him we were going to take the guy off. After all, it was going to be the easiest sixteen ounces we ever scored.

"All you have to do is sit in the back with the baby."

Kasseem then decided that, to cut down on the bullshit and, to avoid any confrontation with the toddler in the car, he would bring a gun just for show. His mother had a 38-caliber revolver in her closet. He retrieved it—fully loaded—and stuck it in his pants. It all made perfect sense. Take a loaded gun to a marijuana rip-off, with a baby in the back seat.

We met the dude as planned but he was really squirrelly and he didn't have the shit. He wanted one of us to come upstairs to the dealer's house with the cash. I did not want to go into the guy's house. Our mark was a lightweight, but the big dealer could have been some kind of badass. Ordinarily, I would have jumped at the chance to meet the source. Maybe cut the middle man out on the next buy. Our target would know that, and I didn't want him to be any more suspicious than he already was. I figured the seller must have been a little nervous too.

"No fuckin way," was my response, "We don't know this guy. What if he tries to rob us?"

Kasseem showed him the flash cash and told him to bring the product to us. Flash cash was a wad of plain paper with a few big bills on either end. It looked like a lot of money, but it wasn't. Of course, he asked us to give him the money first, then he would bring back the product.

"Not happenin'. It's gotta be a hand to hand exchange," I demanded.

The kid was gone a while and when he returned, he only had a half pound. The new proposal was half the pot, half the money, and then the second half of the grass for the balance of the cash. This was the best we were going to do; half a pound is better than nothing at all. But he was still very suspicious. He wouldn't even give us what he had until Kasseem opened the passenger door and let him stick his head in. Kasseem handed the stuff to me. This was it! I threw the shit to CB in the back seat just as Kasseem pulled the gun. We had discussed this before.

"Listen muthah fuckah," I said, "I ain't spending the rest of my days in the joint over a God damned pound of reefer. Don't even load that fuckin gun!"

"Gotta load it man," he said. "If you looking at it from the business end, you can see the bullets. No bullets, no fear. We just gonna scare the muthah fuckah. I ain't shootin nobody with my nephew in that orange car! My man's gonna shit his draws and run like a son of a bitch. Don't worry about it."

Well, the fucking guy saw the gun and just started shrieking. It was like somebody stuck a pencil in his eye or set him on fire.

"No. No. Give me my pot. My pahhht. My pahhht," he wailed.

Holy shit, his screams were ear-piercing. His voice seized the quiet night. The baby was crying, and we had to get out of there. I dropped the stick into drive and started to pull away as he clung to the door still screaming. I slammed on the brakes, sped up, and spun the wheel, trying to shake the kid off the door. Still, he clung there screaming.

"My pahhht. My pahhht!"

Kasseem was pointing the gun yelling, "I'll kill you muthah fucker, I'll kill you." I tried one more maneuver because I realized that Kasseem was on the verge of pulling the trigger. The gun was there to scare the guy; he wasn't supposed to get shot. But there, in that intense moment, in the darkness of that night, the boy was about to die over a half-pound of marijuana and my life was on the verge of ruin. I hit the brakes, grabbed the drugs off the back seat, and threw them out the window. Our boy dove on them like a dog on a steak, and I drove away with Kasseem dishing me a verbal ass-kicking.

"What the fuck is wrong witchoo white boy? We had that shit except for your punk ass."

Actually, I believe he was relieved. He was able to save face on the failed caper by blaming me for the punk-out, and he didn't have to blast the kid. Where would I be now if Kasseem had put a bullet in that young man's face? If little Joey wasn't in the car, things might have gone horribly different. Word got back that the guy was telling people we tried to rob him with a toy gun. He never knew how close he came.

UNDERCOVER FILIBUSTER

I didn't want to give him a chance to say anything. It was just two more blocks and our light was about to turn green. I needed to sound like an asshole.

Detective George Gundlach had joined the Nassau County PD about six months before I did. At twenty-five years old, I was the youngest one in my academy class. I took the entrance exam when I was nineteen. The grading of our test was delayed for years due to a Justice Department investigation into alleged discriminatory hiring practices. Most of us had begun other careers while waiting for Nassau to call. I was working as a security supervisor at Kingsborough Community College in Brooklyn. George Gundlach or Gunlock, as he came to be called, was a locksmith. Supposedly, it was that talent that helped George get some choice assignments through the years. I honestly have no idea whether or not that is true. It was just a rumor, and he was good at what he did. Our paths rarely crossed, Gunlock and mine, until he showed up one summer afternoon at my Precinct. I was working as a Detective Sergeant in the 6th squad in Manhasset. The CO was a lieutenant named Shaun Spillane. Shaun had been, arguably, the best homicide lieutenant in the recent history of the County PD. The show "NYPD Blue" made an episode out of one of his cases.

So, Gunlock shows up with his partner and he tells Spillane and me about this sting they're working on for the DA's squad. There was this wannabe wise guy from Howard Beach who had it in with a mailman in Queens. The mailman was into the bookies and the loan sharks. They told him he had to work off his debt, and they hooked him up with Howard Beach guy. The mailman's job was to steal credit cards out of the mail and give them to Howard Beach guy. Howard Beach Guy would bang out the card for two days and dump it.

Gunlock had an informant who was connected to the Howard Beach guy. At George's request, the informant told Howard Beach guy that he knew a jeweler who was in a jam and needed some money. The plan was that the jeweler would meet Howard Beach guy and pretend to sell him a three-thousand-dollar piece of jewelry. He would only be selling it on paper. The jewelry would be paid for with the stolen credit card, and the jeweler would give Howard Beach guy fifteen hundred bucks, and pocket the other fifteen hundred by billing the credit card company.

With the assistance of one of our squad detectives who worked as security for a jewelry store in Great Neck, Gunlock had convinced the owner to let him use the store as a front for the scam. The owner was going to let Gunlock put an undercover cop in the store pretending to be the jeweler's son, and the son would be the connection.

There were two problems. The jeweler was getting cold feet and he told Gunlock that his undercover could meet with Howard Beach guy and the informant at the store, but the deal would have to go down off-premises. Gunlock figured out a fix for that, but the second speed bump came up when the undercover cop got sick and couldn't make the meet. Since Howard Beach guy was only holding the credit cards for two days, they didn't know when they might get another crack at him. Gunlock didn't want to put the brakes on and risk losing the fish, so he came to us looking for a stand-in to play the jeweler's son. In a squad filled with senior men, I was the only one young enough for the role. I had never done any undercover work before, but I did do some acting in college. I jumped at the opportunity. The 6th precinct was the slowest house in the county and life there was generally dull. Any chance I got to crank up the adrenaline, I grabbed it.

My story would be that I got in over my head with my own credit cards and that I didn't want Daddy to know. When the mark showed up at the store, I would tell him that I had to sneak out and do the deal in a parking lot. I would ask him, and the informant, to wait for me in their car and that I would meet them in ten minutes. The technology of credit card processing has evolved tremendously since then. Every credit card purchase had to be manually swiped on a countertop device that would make an imprint of the card on a carbonized form. Then the storekeeper had to call the credit card company, verify the card was valid, and get a verification number. Gunlock gave me one of the counter-top credit card swipers, and a cellphone to call the credit company. The cell phone was a big bulky unit with a telescoping antenna, but it was cutting edge at the time. It was one step above the old bag phones that many regular people were using. I was surprised he had one. I didn't know our job bought any. I thought those kinds of toys were reserved for elite New York City units and for the Feds, who have unlimited resources. It turned out that I was correct. It wasn't a Nassau Police phone.

The phone and the card swiper were in a shopping bag that I carried out to the informant's Pontiac Grand Prix. I had my 9-millimeter tucked into the back of my pants under my suit jacket. Gunlock said it might blow my cover. I told him to fuck himself and find another undercover. I had no wire and had no backup. Better for me to blow my cover than for Howard Beach guy to blow my brains out. The front passenger seat of the Pontiac was vacant, and I understood that's where they wanted me to sit. *Just as well*, I thought. I never liked sitting in the back of a two-door car with no easy way out when some heavy shit was going down. Besides, if the deal went bad, I could always jump out and run. The informant was driving and he wasn't going to make an effort to stop me. I could be a good distance by the time Howard Beach guy got out of the back seat. I could grab some cover and call 911 on the cell phone. But as I got to the car, I saw that there were two more people in the back. There was a girl in the middle and another man sitting on the right, behind my seat, where I wouldn't be able to see him. This wasn't good.

"We sure have a lot of people in on this," I noted.

"They wanted to go for a ride in the country," said Howard Beach guy. He looked like an actor named Vic Morrow who used to play Sgt. Saunders in a black and white TV series called *Combat*. This guy had the same chiseled granite face topped by a swath of dirty blonde hair. *Probably not pure Italian,* I thought. *Never be a made guy".*

"Where-a we gonna do dis?" he barked from his spot behind the driver.

I directed the informant to the parking lot of Leonard's catering hall on Northern Blvd. The events there are usually at night, so the lot would be empty. I had scoped it out beforehand.

The guy from Howard Beach was burning a hole in my face with his eyes. I was watching the road as I was giving directions and avoided looking at him, but I felt his glare.

"What's going on? You and Pops not getting along?" He was feeling me out.

"My relationship with my father should not concern you," I was trying to sound a little nerdy. I was trying to sound like a jeweler's son. "Here it is. We can do it here."

"Da fella dat owns dis place knows people," Howard Beach guy was talking to the man behind me. He was talking about Leonard's. He was making reference to the fact that he was familiar with the place and that the owner was allegedly acquainted with some important people in the world of Howard Beach wannabe mobsters. The man behind me didn't respond. He was making me very uncomfortable. As the car was coming to a stop, I squinted and pulled down my windshield visor as matter-of-factly as I could. I was actually hoping there would be a mirror there so I could see the guy behind me. I was disappointed when I found it was hidden by a flip-up cover.

"You awright?" asked the guy from Howard Beach.

"Yeah, it's just a little bright. Okay, three thousand dollars. That's the deal, right? I have to put the tax on it."

"No problem. Here's da card. Ya know, I might like to get something from your joint for my girl here."

I ignored him while I pulled the swiper device from the shopping bag and swiped the card. I practiced it at the station house to be sure I didn't look like it was my first time doing it. It came out well, so I wrote the amount on the slip, $3000 + tax $247.50 = $3247.50. Then, I reached for the phone. I yanked the credit card clearance telephone number out of my pocket. I had it written on the back of a business card from the jewelry store along with the store's code number. I held up the phone and started to dial.

"What the fuck is dat? Property of the FBI?" Howard Beach guy's voice had taken on a slightly different tone, but he was still very calm. I wasn't. I twisted that fat fucking cell phone around and there it was: a white sticker with black bold letters, "PROPERTY OF THE FBI."

I had been in some tight spots before, but this one was really tense. The rule of the three B's in police work dictates that the best cops have three common traits Brains, Balls, and Brawn in order of importance. A good cop will have two of the three: Brains and Balls or Brains and Brawn. When you're a skinny little white kid, growing up in the street like I did, you learn to survive using the most powerful weapon you have, your brain. If you can't beat 'em with brawn, baffle 'em with bullshit! But you better have the balls to pull it off.

One afternoon in the early 70s, I found myself riding home from the Bronx on the D train. Why I was in the Bronx alone that day, I cannot recall. I've done stupider things. Sitting with my back to the sliding door leading to the next subway car, I was facing the far end of the car I was in. There was a handful of people on the train, but the subways were ravaged by crime at that time. The hoodlums would rob multiple people at once and police protection was sparse.

We were somewhere between the 125th Street stop and the 59th Street stop. That was a very long trip between stops with nowhere to get off. There I was—lazily gazing around the car reading the graffiti. You couldn't see out the windows because there was so much graffiti. A lot of it was gang graffiti. Dirty Dozens, Black Spades, Seven Immortals, Peacemakers, Black Pearls, Savage Skulls, Turbans, Young Sinners, Royal Javelins, Dutchmen, Magnificent Seven, Ghetto Brothers.

There was also something written there about the Hoe Avenue Peace Meeting. The Hoe Avenue Peace Meeting is a legendary meeting of ten or twelve clicks in the Bronx. It was supposedly called by a local gang social worker to propose a general peace pact and a kind of inter-gang alliance. I bet the cops loved that idea, one huge street gang all over the city. The impetus for the meeting was the murder of 'Black Benjie,' a leader of the Ghetto Brothers gang. Of course, it didn't work out. We had heard something about it back in Queens, but we figured it was bullshit. A lot of the story now is folklore. There was a movie called *The Warriors* that was loosely based on the event. Good flick.

As I sat there reading the walls, the pass-through door at the other end slid open and three vicious-looking young men stepped in from the next car. One of them was markedly shorter than the other two. Short guys often have something to prove. That can make them very dangerous.

"Look here muthah fuckahs, y'all know what this is. Now give it up," the little guy shouted.

Fucking train robbery, I thought.

One of the other passengers got right up and turned to come my way. I guess he thought he would try to escape.

"Sit yaw ass down white boy," the hood demanded. And he did.

The marauders then began soliciting 'contributions.' A lady took her wallet out of her purse and gave it to one of them. He pulled out the bills and dropped the wallet on the floor. Some guy handed his cash to another. Then some dope refused.

"What? No? Get Bucky," boomed the short guy. Instantly one of the others retreated to the car they just came out of.

I guess he's going to get Bucky, I thought. Good guess. Those guys were my age, but they were super hardcore. When Bucky came in, he had to duck through the doorway. He was one big kid.

"Yo Bucky, this kid don't wanna give it up."

The little punk gestured toward a young, collegiate-looking Asian man who had a nervously defiant look about him. Without a word, Bucky stepped up and nailed the poor guy square in his face. The kid's nose basically exploded. Two of the others resumed collection, while Bucky and his cohort rifled the poor broken-nosed dude's pockets. The blood on the window blended right in with the colorful graffiti.

The short kid was coming my way. Two more of them had come in behind Bucky. Fighting and running were both out of the question. The train was too short, and I was alone. Either option would have had the same result, serious injuries for me. Of course, I was the last one in that car. Even if I gave it up, there was no guarantee I wouldn't get my ass whipped just for the hell of it. This was it.

"How bout choo man? What-choo got?"

"Naw man, you don't wanna take me off."

"What? Yo Bucky!"

I gave a quick look. Bucky and the other two were busy fucking with some other guy.

"Yo, Homie, hold up now. I didn't say you couldn't take me off, I just said you didn't want to."

My guy was momentarily stunned by the way I spoke. Not like a white kid. I figured that time was my friend. The train felt like it was going in slow motion, but I knew that was in my mind. 59th Street couldn't be too far now and these guys would have to bail out at that spot and take off.

"What the fuck you talkin about?"

He straightened slightly and gave me just a little space. For just an instant, I thought about kicking him in the balls. Just for an instant. That would have been the wrong move. I sensed I had an edge when he backed off, and I had to keep the momentum.

"Check it out, man. I'm down witch y'all. I do what y'all bruthahs do, but I'm just off today. I ain't like these other honky muthah fuckahs."

He was listening.

"I'm just sayin, I was up in the Bronx today. I went up there to see my old lady. Check out, my boys." I pointed to my shoes. I was wearing my Playboys. White people didn't wear Playboys.

He took a step back and really looked at me. He looked me up and he looked me down.

"I'm too clean man. Am I right?"

The others had begun to move toward us.

"You went to see yo old lady? Where at?"

"Tremont Avenue. Her bruthah took a bid today and she was all sad and shit. But the bitch had her period! You believe that shit?"

"Where the fuck you from white boy?"

"Brooklyn," I lied. Queens might have gotten me a beating on general principals.

"Wassup with this one," Bucky demanded.

The moment had come. I was out of time and out of options. No more bullshit. *They might not only take my money, but they might take my Playboys too,* I thought.

"Naw Bucky, he awright man. Muthah fuckah's like a White bruthah. Check him out."

"Awright. C'mon. Let's get the fuck outa here."

And that was that. Bucky yanked the door handle, slid it open, and stepped through to the next car. The others followed and they were gone. I saw them bounding up the stairs at the 59th Street station. Someone helped the poor exploded nosed guy off the train, the doors closed, and we headed on out to 42nd Street where I would change to the 7th train and head on home. These were true survival skills you don't learn in school.

Back in the parking lot at Leonard's Great Neck, things had gotten real sketchy. I could feel the tension in the Pontiac as I turned that cell phone around and spotted that God damned sticker.

How the fuck did this happen? was my thought.

I twisted a little in my seat so I could see the guy behind me in my peripheral vision, and I held the phone up high in my left hand with the sticker facing the back seat. As all eyes shot to the phone, I slid my hand onto the butt of my pistol.

"Holy shit! Property of the FBI," I laughed. "You guys probably think I'm a cop or something!"

I was still smiling as I lowered fucking Gunlock's Fed phone. I knew my job didn't have toys like this. No one else was smiling.

"Take it easy guys; I'm a jeweler, not a cop. My BMW was stolen a few months ago and this phone was in the car. The FBI recovered it in a shipping crate, heading for South America with a bunch of other cars. The phone had the sticker on it when I got it back, and I never took it off."

I actually surprised myself. *Where did that come from?* I wondered.

"I'd have to be a pretty dumb cop to have that on there. Am I right?" I asked everyone in general.

Nobody else spoke a word. The guy from Howard Beach just stared at me.

I had to keep the momentum going my way, the same as I did on the D train so many years before.

"All right, let me make this call."

No one spoke. I made the call and cleared the card.

"Great. That worked out. Here you go, fifteen hundred." I counted out fifteen one hundred dollar bills.

I handed the cash to Howard Beach guy, but he didn't take it. He didn't even look at it. He just stared at me. I felt like my eyes were on fire.

"Gimmee a copy of da slip," he said calmly.

"The slip?"

"Yeah! I wanna see the fuckin slip."

I complied.

"I just wanna be sure you ain't rippin me off," he perused the slip.

"Okay, three grand plus tax. Gimmee da cash."

He put out his hand, I laid the hundred dollar bills on his palm, and he counted it. He counted it without looking at it. He just kept glaring at me.

"I should make you gimme half the tax too."

"That all goes to the government one way or the other," I answered.

"Lucky you don't get yourself hurt with that God damned sticker, jeweler."

"Sorry man. Let's go. I have to get back to the shop. The old man is going to start asking questions."

The informant already had his Grand Prix in the drive, and we were moving.

After a few blocks, the guy from Howard Beach broke the silence.

"So, I might wanna get something for my girl here. You got Rolex?"

"Of course, we have Rolex! What kind of jewelry store would we be if we didn't carry Rolex?"

He gazed out the window for a few moments and without looking back at me he asked, "What about Piaget? You got Piaget?"

Shit, I thought. "*Piaget? What the fuck is Piaget?*

It turned out that Piaget is a high-end watch, but I had never heard of it.

Is he trying to set me up? If I said yes, I could be alright, but this might be a test. If he made up that name, Piaget, I failed and I could be fucked. The store was close now, and I had to buy some time. I'd go on a filibuster.

"Look mister, I'm in a little debt right now and this should straighten things out for me. It's not going to happen again and I can never see myself doing anything like this again. Nothing personal, but after today I really don't want to see you or any of you guys again."

I didn't want to give him a chance to say anything. It was just two more blocks and our light was about to turn green. I needed to sound like an asshole.

"If we all met someplace else, some other time, I'm sure we could have been friends, but after doing this, I don't think I could hold it together. You understand what I mean."

I looked at the girl and she nodded.

"I'm sure you're all very nice people and all, but …"

The car had stopped in front of the jewelry store.

"Awright already. Stop cryin' and get the fuck out! Jesus Christ."

That was the only thing the guy behind me said the whole time.

I did what he said and the car pulled away.

Detective Gunlock and I had a private discussion about his major league screw up. I was pissed, but I was also pumped. I was really thrilled by the way I handled that incident. I still had the golden tongue. I told the story to Spillane and the other squad dicks, but I promised Gunlock I wouldn't mention it to his boss. Later on, the informant told Gunlock that he was amazed at the way it went.

Brains and balls, baby. Brains and balls.

WHY ME?

*Does anyone know where the love of God goes
when the waves turn the minutes to hours?*

—Gordon Lightfoot

When I first made Detective Sergeant, I was reassigned from the First to the Fourth Precinct. I had been a cop there, and I was excited about the chance to work with some of my old honchos. Unfortunately, it didn't work out as well as I had hoped. Some of the older guys in the squad were resentful. I made it there on a hook. A hook was like a *rabbi* or a connection to someone with juice. Don't get me wrong, I had the qualifications. I was a working street cop and a working street sergeant. I earned two medals and a couple of 'Cop of the Month' awards before I was made supervisor. Then, I went over to the First Precinct which was arguably the busiest Nassau County had to offer. I spent two years in the street there.

The fact was, nobody went to 'the dicks' as we called the detective squad, without a hook. My dream had been an assignment to Narcotics. I got out hooked for that spot. Now, my stigma was that I had out hooked some senior guys for my precinct squad position in the Fourth, and that caused me some problems having only seven years on the job and no detective experience.

There was one particular detective at the Fourth Squad when I got there. I will call him Detective X. Detective X and I had both worked in the Fourth Precinct when we were cops. Some guys referred to Detective X as an empty suit. That meant that he wore the uniform, but he never did anything in it. There were super cops who took care of their posts, assisted other cops on calls, were proactive, and were always anxious to immerse themselves in police work. There was also the middle of the road guys who did what was expected of them and then did their own thing. Some had side businesses. Others had girlfriends on their posts, but in general, when the bell rang, they would come out of their corners and do the job. Then there were the empty suits. The guys who made work avoidance into an art form. They would do only the bare minimum, hideout on the night tours, and sign on meal break when the guy on the next post needed assistance with a DWI or some other unpleasant or dangerous situation. The empty suits came in all shapes sizes and colors. Detective X happened to be black.

Detective X got into the detective division on his own hook a few years earlier than I, and the other squad dicks were carrying him. He was assigned to my squad and his work was totally unacceptable from the start. I let him know about it regularly, but I kept it between us as long as I could. The problem was that I had to keep riding him. He was getting pissed because I insisted that he pull his weight. And I was taking a huge gamble by not writing him up. I knew it could come back to bite me and I was right.

When Detective X dropped the ball on following up on a possible abduction investigation, I had to inform the squad CO. The CO chewed Detective X a new asshole, but that was the end of it. Neither of us wrote him up. When Detective X fucked up again, it was the same story. There was a lot of yelling and ultimatums, but no formal discipline and no written record of either incident. Big mistake on my part. Detective X set out to bring me down.

One chilly night in the fall, a call came from downstairs. Detective X was squealing. That meant he was up for assignment to any new case referred by the uniformed desk officer (D.O.) to the detective squad. The D.O. called to tell us that a five-year-old white child had told his parents that their black female housekeeper had sexually assaulted him. The housekeeper was assigned to the family by the Department of Social Services. This meant that the family was dysfunctional in some way. Furthermore, they lived in an old-time, lower-middle class Caucasian enclave called Island Park. Detective X told me he was going to call the family in at 8 p.m. with the child for an interview. He was trying to take the easy way out, and I knew why. For one thing, he was lazy. But this was also going to be a particularly uncomfortable assignment for him. Detective X was black. The victim and family were white. The alleged perpetrator was black. It was an old, blue-collar, white red neck neighborhood. Detective X wanted to conduct business in his own house, so to speak. I could relate to that, but it was the wrong way to go with this. It was late. The child would likely be frightened and intimidated by our police dominated neon light atmosphere. The place to investigate this complaint was right in the little boy's home at the scene of the allegations, not to mention the fact that there may have been a crime scene. Detective X was unconvinced, and I had to order him to do it the way it needed to be done. Not being insensitive to his own plight, I added, "And make sure you take somebody with you in case the family gives you a hard time or the kid doesn't want to talk to you." Who could have known how this logical and seemingly innocuous directive would turn itself around on me? He did what I ordered and left with a White Detective partner.

When they got back, and after he briefed me on the investigation, Detective X looked at me and demanded, "What did you mean when you said, take somebody with you in case he doesn't want to talk to me?"

"Well," I replied, "In case he didn't want to talk to you or the parents gave you some shit because you're black, you'd have somebody there with you to back you up. To make sure we got the job done."

And there began the most stressful and difficult time of my entire twenty-eight-year-long career with the Nassau County Police Department. Detective X started ranting about making assignments based on race.

"That's totally racist, Sarge. You can't make assignments based on race."

"First of all," I said, again responding with logic, "I didn't make this assignment based on race. You caught the squeal. I didn't take it away from you. But I made you take a partner to cover your ass. Secondly, the job had to get done. That's the most important thing. It wasn't going to get done the way you wanted to do it, and that's what you're really pissed off about. Now don't try to turn it around on me."

He did.

He rallied together with the 'Guardians,' the black police officer's association and they lobbied the police department to have me demoted as a racist. Can you imagine that? Me? They called me a racist. Yet I had simply observed that the detective, and the job he was duty-bound to perform, might themselves fall victim to racism, real racism.

In truth, the scrutiny I bore was a result of my belief that we needed to remain impervious to such ignorance. As defenders of the defenseless, we had a mission to accomplish. Failure was never an option. Success was mandatory despite the sociological obstacles. If that meant sucking it up, we had to suck it up. People throw garbage and feces at the police. They spit on us and they curse us. It is our resourcefulness and cool response that allows us to prevail. If the child wouldn't talk to a black detective, we would give him a white detective. Or a Hispanic. Or an Asian. We do what we have to do to get the job done. We suck it up. I was thirty-one years old and vaulted back to the painful reality of my youthful identity crisis. I still wasn't black, and nothing I had done fifteen years before could now save me from this lynch mob. The investigation of the detective's allegations hung over my head for about six months. Talk about stress! I tried to explain that Detective X was a 'zero.' That he was motivated to attack me because I had been riding him. Lieutenant

Engels got amnesia and with no documentary evidence, I had no defense. They failed to get me demoted, but I was fined several days' pay and transferred to the slowest precinct squad in the County of Nassau. This is the kind of bullshit that really pisses me off. There's plenty of genuine hatred in this country. Real racism needs to be addressed. This kind of crap is just a distraction from the genuine problems. The situation only gets worse when something like this happens to someone like me. Everyone knew this was a railroad job and it pissed a lot of people off, but no one had the balls to step up and put the brakes on it. The bosses were too concerned about their own careers to put a stop to this injustice. It was politically charged. A hot potato! The worst part about it is that I was stigmatized. The official charges said, "Detective Sergeant Lowry made racially insensitive comments in making an assignment."

There was, however, a silver lining. I appealed my case to the Disciplinary Review Board. This was a group of five of the highest-ranking chiefs in the department, including the four-star Chief of Department. It was an intimidating group for a young supervisor to face. After much rehearsal, I made a professional presentation. I told them exactly what happened. When they asked me if, given the chance, I would do it over again I answered, "Chiefs, as the squad supervisor I had a mission. That mission was to ensure that the allegations made by the complainant were adequately and safely investigated. So yes, I would do the same thing again. The only thing I would change is that I wouldn't tell the detective why I wanted him to take the other guy with him. His actions were borderline insubordinate. I gave him an order and that's all he needed to know."

That impressed them. They didn't reduce my charges, but they could have bumped them up. They didn't do that either. And a couple of them actually caught me privately and commended me for my professionalism. Suddenly, the most influential people in the department knew my name. They knew I was a guy that could be counted on to get the job done. That stuck with me and with them.

For the rest of my career, I always did what I thought was right regardless of the possible consequences. I never put on a show. I was always myself. This is who I am, take it, or leave it.

As a chief, being myself was a problem. I wasn't like the other chiefs. Chiefs were supposed to act a certain way and dress a certain way. I called them 'cookie-cutter bosses.' I was different. I never took things too seriously. I never stressed over anything, but I always got the job done. That pissed some people off. Cops get nervous around other cops who dance to a different tune, especially when the dancer is successful. I spent five years as an adolescent trying to be something I wasn't. It almost destroyed me. I was never going to do that again. I had to be true to myself. I had to be me. I have been ferociously individualistic my entire adult life, regardless of anyone's opinion.

The Detective X event also reminded me of how racism cuts both ways. After I got transferred, a high-ranking officer came up to me at a party. He was hammered drunk. He said, "Yo Spike, I heard they bounced you to the Sixth Squad. At least there's no niggers up there to bust your balls."

This was the stigma I would now have to live with. I said, "Boss, please don't talk to me like that. I despise that word. You have to understand that the thing was never about race. The guy is an empty suit. That's what it was about. You know how it works. I rode him to get him to do his job. He saw a chance to fuck me, and he took it. A white guy would have done the same thing in his position; it just would have come from another angle."

"You got it, Spike," he smacked me on the back.

He was only kidding around with me, but it made me think long and hard about stereotypes. The kids I ran with were all criminals. But they weren't criminals because they were black or Hispanic, any more than I was a criminal because I was white. What we all had in common is that we were all born into some kind of fucked up situation. So we gravitated to the street. And there's an anger in the street that grows out of the pain and despair experienced by people born into fucked up situations. That anger breeds hatred and that hatred is best directed at a common enemy. Having a common enemy unites people.

It can be a complex dynamic like the people in one housing project hating the people in the project across the street. Or it can be as simple as hating someone for the color of his or her skin.

Just look at how well people across the country got along after September 11th. Suddenly, we had a common enemy. It was short-lived, but it was the first time I saw people talking about themselves as Americans rather than Irish, Italian, African-Americans, etc. This is also something that fuels gangs. Kids join gangs for protection, they join for adventure, and they join to be a part of something: to bond. That bonding becomes tighter when they find a common enemy.

So, it's no wonder that I gravitated to police work. The Police Department is a big, well organized, and well-paid gang. We offer protection, adventure, and an opportunity to be part of something. We even wear colors. And we have a common enemy, the bad guys.

"The criminal law is about blaming someone." That's what I teach my criminal justice students at Molloy College. When something goes wrong, someone has to take the heat. Human beings need to release the rage that's born of sorrow, pain, despair, and just about any other spate of unpleasantness. Blaming ourselves simply compounds the fracture. This phenomenon becomes quite evident in the course of suicide investigations. The decedent's survivors prefer theories of murder to the realization of the suicide. This is often in direct contradiction to the overwhelming evidence to the contrary and, at times, even in the face of a suicide note.

The Sixth Squad Detectives was a dull assignment. The only action I ever saw there was on county duty. Every week, a different detective sergeant was assigned responsibility for the night shift countywide. On one such night, we got a call for a body in a van. The body turned out to be a man with a bullet in his head and a pistol on the floor. The doors were locked, the handgun was his, and there was a suicide note.

"I think the killer made him write that note," was the response from his closest family member.

That's what family members often do in suicide cases. They prefer it to be murder rather than suicide. "It had to be murder. He never would have done this." The alternative, suicide, can lead to the often equally irrational conclusion that "The death was my fault. I missed the signs. I should have done more." It's healthy to get pissed off at someone else. And it can't be the dead guy because he was a beloved family member. Victims need someone to hate, someone to blame. Then there is no guilt, only catharsis. So, in the case of suicide, it may be a phantom slayer.

But who is at fault for the criminality of a teenage boy? Who can *he* blame for his delinquent plight? His friends? His parents? Society? Maybe God himself? In his lyrics from 'The Wreck of the Edmund Fitzgerald,' Gordon Lightfoot implies that God may have abandoned the twenty-nine sailors, on the ill-fated freighter as it sank in the frigid November winds of the Great Lakes. For the wives and the sons and the daughters of those men, only one of two conclusions could be drawn. Either God turned his back on them, or the mariners fucked up and got killed. The latter is unacceptable.

So, what happened to me? Who was responsible for the creation of Kevin Lowry, that confused and depraved young punk who committed just about every sin his Catholic school teachers warned him against? The answer, of course, is Kevin Lowry. I moved long ago, beyond the blaming stage. No child criminal was ever forced into delinquency. We all did, however, make our choices based upon a myriad of psychological, sociological, and physiological factors and events outside of our control, which predictably predisposed us or even prompted us to gravitate in the wrong direction. Like fingerprints and snowflakes, we are all distinct. No two children become the products of exactly the same experiences. At the same time, most young hoodlums share some common core influences. In the course of my introspection, I came across a number of specific factors that shaped me into the boy I was, and the man I ultimately became.

ADRENALINE JUNKY

Before having children of my own, I rejected any idea that children are born with predispositions. My belief was that personalities are formed completely based on the input of the immediate family and household. That could not have been more incorrect. Babies are born with unique personalities. No doubt, household influence is powerful. So much so, in fact, that it can alter a child's disposition. But, if left unaffected, certain personality traits initiated at birth will become permanent. When I was about six or seven years old, my parents took me to the local RKO Theater to see *West Side Story*. The RKO theaters were a magnificent chain of entertainment facilities located throughout the city of New York. Opening in the 20s, these theaters hosted everything from vaudeville to Shaft. Most were three-story extravaganzas created in art decor, or Spanish Baroque styling, with crystal chandeliers, fine carpeting, ushers, and full balcony seating. They featured only one screen, but going to the movies was a vacation-like experience.

West Side Story instantly became my favorite movie and even now, remains one of my top ten. I actually played the role of 'Action' in a college production of the show. Coincidence? I don't think so. But as a child, I fancied myself a first-grade member of the Jets street gang. My mother bought the record album of the soundtrack and, when it played, I would dance around the living room tossing and catching a black-handled rubber knife with a floppy silver blade. A few years later, I ordered myself a leather wristband from the Johnson Smith catalog. It had two straps and two buckles, just like the ones the Sharks wore in the movie. I wore it every day.

Excitement was what I craved more than ice cream! Good grades came easy for me in grammar school, but I had a short attention span. Inevitably, boredom would drive me to make something happen. The other kids began to count on me to stir up some shit and I never failed to accommodate them. This led to regular detention and frequent parent-teacher conferences. I landed a few suspensions, but maneuvering close to the edge without going over never got expelled. I needed more action and I found it on the street. It seemed like the black kids were always into something fun. I was ready to graduate from bike races around the block, and toy soldier wars with my white friends. Their numbers were dwindling anyway. That, coupled with the fact that I was getting my ass whipped by the brothers on a semi-periodic basis, prompted me to join up. This was a critical juncture. Emphasis should be placed here on the fact that there was a duel motivator at play. Joining a gang for protection alone is extremely common. Most kids though are already seeking something else like family, money, and more intense experiences.

It has been theorized and often espoused that drug users become quickly dissatisfied and are on a constant search for a bigger and better high. Adrenaline is a form of natural drug produced by the body. Those of us who become hooked, or are born with an adrenaline-starved predisposition, always crave a bigger and better rush. Thus, it follows that a person achieving that rush by means of criminal activity would have to perpetually raise the danger bar in order to continue to achieve maximum satisfaction. And that is what we did.

PARENTAL ATTENTION

Simultaneous to the hunt for a more eventful lifestyle, I was experiencing the pain of the marital discord and outright violence taking place in my home. My descent from the focus of attention to the status of a piece of bric-a-brac was so rapid that it could have made my ears pop. With the exception of an occasional, "Oh poor Kevin. Look what we're doing to our son," I went largely unnoticed until I did something to grab their attention. Getting arrested or seriously banged up in a fight would accomplish just that, albeit temporarily.

In my subconscious, anti-social behavior also had the effect of drawing my parents closer to one another. If I became the problem, Mimi and Semmes would be forced to unite and address the issue, thereby shifting their focus off from their private war and making them allies in mine.

Naturally, all of this was taking place in a part of my brain to which I had no direct access at that time. Adolescent boys use remarkably little of their brainpower. This analysis unfolded over time as I watched my criminal life grow smaller in my cerebral rearview mirror.

BODY CHANGES

Adolescence is a tumultuous time, with lasagna layers of confusion and emotional challenges, not the least of which is the effect of multiple, rapid physical body changes. When a teenager looks in the mirror, he sees an unfamiliar person, inside and out. There is a new size, pimples, hair where it never was, and all sorts of strange things happening in his head and his pants. Most boys are embarrassed, uncomfortable, and a little frightened by their strange new selves. They feel a need to hide from the public at large, while at the same time being compelled to make their mark among their peers. This explains their obsession with fads in clothing. Fad clothing acts as teenage camouflage, allowing a boy to disappear in the crowd. Effectively, the boy becomes part of a well-defined group while hiding among its members. Both the need to belong and the need to be publicly unobtrusive are fulfilled.

This was obviously unachievable for me. I could never be totally like them, and I was the single most obtrusive person in the group. My father coined me the snowflake in the mud puddle; always the first to be seen and the first to get hit.

MR. WEST

There are eight million people in this city. If seven million hate your guts, you still have a million friends.

It happened on Halloween. It was a Saturday, so we started early. Wandering around town with our eggs and shaving cream, we got shitfaced on pot and Bali High wine from a seventy-nine cent pocket rocket. It was a free for all. By the time it ended, we, and anyone who crossed our paths, got doused with yokes and foam. But as the Sun got shy and started to hide behind the high-rises, the air turned cold. Jose and I were not prepared and we got chilly. As we passed Klein's department store, we came up with a logical solution. "Let's stop in here and pick up a couple of leather jackets."

We were stoned, full of cheap wine, and overconfident in our ability to steal. All cocky and arrogant, without any of our normal reconnaissance or diversionary tactics, he and I just strolled on in there, put on a couple of coats, and walked out. When we got busted, we struggled with the store detectives and they took us down hard. That was totally out of character for us. No planning. No lookout. Just grab and boogie. We bought ourselves an express ticket to the 109 Precinct. For me, it ended with a probation sentence and a shrink.

I got assigned to Mr. Ed West. He was a veteran black probation officer, working out of an office on Sutphin Boulevard in Jamaica Queens. He had seen every kind of hood come through there and nobody, no, nobody was going to bullshit Ed West. He was a hard ass, but despite all the crap, he was a deeply dedicated man and he had a desperate desire to rescue the precious few savable boys that came his way. Mr. West saw something in me and he went to work.

It took him only a few sessions before he read me like a dime novel.

"What the fuck's wrong with you boy? There ain't a God damned thing wrong with being right. You could be right. You want to be right, correct?"

"Yes," I said it and I really meant it. Just about this time was when we went on our Hill boy hunt. I was in grave danger. I wanted out.

"So why in the hell you tryin so hard to be wrong?"

Those words gonged in my brain like the Liberty bell.

"Why in the hell you tryin' so hard to be wrong?"

I spent about three months exploring that issue with Mr. West. I was straight up with him all the time. No point in trying to bullshit Mr. West. He always knew what time it was.

The weekly meetings with the shrink, on the other hand, were a waste of time. That was just for the benefit of my court appearances. That guy did nothing for me. He was a book taught psychologist who knew nothing about where I was coming from. Mr. West was a street guy. He pegged my act from day one. Ed West had seen me before in the faces of countless others. He knew what I needed and before long, I came to know it too.

He said, "Boy, you have no self-confidence. You are so worried about being liked; you forgot how to be yourself. There are eight million people in this city. If seven million hate your guts, you still have a million friends."

I never forgot that, and I have been true to myself since.

"There are eight million people in this city. If seven million hate your guts, you still have a million friends."

At our next meeting, I finally brought it up. We were discussing my neighborhood.

"Mr. West, I gotta get the fuck outta there. If I stay there, I'm going down."

His poker face never betrayed his hand.

"So, what are you gonna do?"

"I'm gonna ask my parents to move."

That was the first day of the rest of my life. He agreed, and that's what I did. I sat down with my parents that night and I told them what we had to do. I told them that if we didn't leave that neighborhood, I would not survive. I would be doomed to a life of crime and punishment. I also asked Mr. West to call them. God bless Mimi and Semmes. They listened to me. They listened to him. They believed in me. They took a moment to step back from their own issues and they agreed to move. Of course, this was no fairy tale. There wouldn't be a house in the country. Economic reality dictated. If we moved out, we could only go far enough to put a little asphalt between me and my demise. I would have to do the rest. I promised to set the boundaries and we struck a deal. There could be no turning back. I had to make myself disappear. We wouldn't be far away, but in New York City, a lot can change in a mile. Breaking the news to 'The Family' would require some skillful planning.

The next day, I laid it on the line. Kasseem and Robazz were key. If I won them over, the rest would go along. We were in the clubhouse in the basement chillin and puffing some reefer. Typical. When Thumper left, I ripped off the bandaid.

"Fellas," I started, "I gotta lay some heavy shit down on ya."

"What's up white boy," Kasseem asked, sucking down some smoke and passing the joint to his younger sibling.

"I'm movin'."

"What the fuck you talkin about?" Robazz actually jumped to his feet.

"It's real man." I looked at the floor and shook my head with feigned despair. "My parents are looking to move to Hempstead."

Hempstead was a black neighborhood in Long Island. It was still important to me that they believed I would be unchanged. I needed them to think that I would still be 'cool.' So, I picked a place that they could accept and one that was far enough away that they would never visit.

"Hempstead! Fuckin Hempstead?" Kasseem snorted. "That's God damned far, niggah."

Everybody just sat quietly for a while, mulling it all over. Robazz just stared at me for a while. I swear to this day, he saw through me. I believe he knew that I was doing what I had to do. He knew I had to go. He always seemed to think that there was something else for me. He should have thought that about himself. He was a smart kid with a lot of charisma. He would have made a great cop. We often fanaticized about us being partners in the NYPD together and all the fun we would have playing for the other team.

Finally, Robazz stood up again. He walked over to me and put his hand on my shoulder. I looked in his eyes and he said, "It's cool out there man. You gonna be awright."

That's all I needed. It was a done deal. The problem was that it wasn't going to happen overnight. I would be expected to keep hanging with the click until moving day, whenever that was going to be.

CHENEE'

*Wherever she is today, she probably has no idea about
the importance of the role she played in my life.*

henee' Gardenhire was a gang chick. I'd known her since before she had
tits. She grew up in the B wing of the Regency House. Over the years, she
gravitated toward the Latinos. So, when the Screaming Phantoms came to
town, it was a natural fit for her. She went out with a couple of the guys in the
click, and she wound up having a bad experience with one of them. The dude's

name was Jose. He grew up in the neighborhood, but he was a little older than most of us. He went to Vietnam and when he came back, he slid in with the Phantoms. He had changed from before he left. He wasn't the same guy. Most Vets were different when they came back. I don't know exactly what happened between Jose and Chenee', but I know it left her shaken and looking to get out. The problem is, nobody gets out. You can't just stop showing up. The only way to get out is to get away.

The timing couldn't have been better. I had already decided to get away. My real family, my parents and I, were moving to 'Hempstead.' That had been firmly established. The boys were okay with it and I falsely promised to come back often. But the move wasn't set. Mimi and Semmes had to find another place cheap enough for them to afford, and they would have to break their lease where we were. There would be an indefinite amount of time to kill. And that's all I wanted to kill. I didn't want to kill anybody and I didn't want anybody to kill me while I was waiting to be paroled from my life. Chenee' was the answer to my dilemma, as I was to hers. In fact, our romance proved to be more than either one of us expected. We didn't plan for it to happen. She was free, I was free, and we just started talking. It didn't take long for things to heat up. Chenee' was sweet and fine; and I showed her a soft streak that she found irresistible. The word was mum for a while, but people started catching the wind. Before long, Robazz brought it up.

"Yo man, you been hangin tough with that Phantom babe lately."

"Not really man," I responded with caution.

"Yeah, you have you honky muthah fuckah! You should go for that shit man."

"Really?"

"Fuckin A straight. That be good for everybody round here. Be like a merger between us and the spicks. You never know when some shit might jump off with those fuckin Phantoms. Mother fuckers doing acid all the time.

Bein' tight with them keeps most of these other assholes the fuck outta here and leaves us to do our shit. Ya dig what I'm sayin?"

"Yeah man," I said with repressed delight, "I'm down with that."

"The only thing is like what's up with her and Jose?" Robazz showed some concern.

"Naa man, that shits over. He quit her."

I really wasn't sure where Jose was at with this, but I took a gamble.

"Cool then. Jump!"

That was the blessing I needed. Both sides condoned the relationship and, in fact, they eased off some of the pressure on us to hang out with them. As the symbol of the alliance between the clicks, we were left pretty much alone as long as we were with each other and we stayed with each other all the time. But Chenee' was more than just a hideout for me. Wherever she is today, she probably has no idea about the importance of the role she played in my life. She gave me just what I needed. Chenee' restored my self-confidence. She made me believe in myself again. She loved me for who I was. There was no need to play a role with Chenee'. She just liked being with Kevin. I didn't know it at the time but I needed that positive reinforcement. I needed it desperately.

I hung with Chenee' and went to see Mr. West twice a week. I didn't have to see him that much, but it was another excuse to get away for a while. Then there was school and the shrink, and I made it all work. I stayed off the radar and out of harm's way.

As the moving day came closer, I started feeling the pain for Chenee'. The old man saw it coming. He kept telling me, "You're getting too close to this girl. You know, we're getting outta here. Somebody's goin to get hurt."

Leading up to our last day was an odd time. Knowing I had to go, and knowing I would have to leave her, had drawn me into a kind of fantasy limbo. As much as I adored her for saving me, I knew I could never be truly saved unless I left her. She knew it too. We had no secrets. Our passion carried the weight of the pain that had to come. I asked her to come with me, but she said she had to make her own way, and she couldn't leave her mom.

When the date was set and I broke the news, she just turned away and said, "Go." One word. One syllable. It stands out in my mind among all of the frightful moments I experienced there, in that nightmare world, as one of my most painful. "Go."

I went, and despite my father's greatest fear, I never went back.

But the pain I was feeling was not just for Chenee. I loved those boys too. We were tight. We shared a bizarre bond built on friendship and rules. And I loved the street. I knew I had to be a cop. My efforts through recent years, to locate Chenee' have proven fruitless. The gate in the wall opened in front of me and quickly closed behind. She was left locked inside. So many nights, I have prayed that she was able to make a better life for herself. I have searched for her just so I could tell her what a tremendous contribution she made not only to me but to those whose lives I may have touched during my journey. The same goes for Probation Officer Ed West. My children are forever in their debt, yet they will never know each other. Surely, Mr. West is dead now and he died without knowing what he had accomplished. Such is the plight of those who choose that profession. Probation is a thankless and unheralded business that commands my highest respect. How fitting it was then for me to have the honor to command the Nassau County Probation Dept. for three years during my police career. The Officers I worked with there could have no clue as to the secret I carried, and the admiration I had for all of them. That time ranks among the highest lights of my life.

Mimi and Semmes moved us to a place, not in Hempstead but Queens, a short ten-minute drive from the corner of Sanford Avenue and Frame Place. But it might as well have been another state. It felt like freedom, not just for me, but for them too. Taking them out of there allowed them to begin to heal. Only now I realize that it wasn't just me that was saved. They were saved too. We took a two-bedroom apartment in a two-family semi-attached home in Bayside. It was owned by an elderly Jewish couple who lived downstairs. A blanket of normalcy immediately shrouded the three of us, and my parents began relating to each other again. We were living there in Bayside, the fateful night I met my life's love. There she was skating around at the Roller Palace in Sheepshead Bay in Brooklyn. It was March 10th, 1979. She knocked some spinning Guido flat on his ass, and I knew at that moment that Ann Elizabeth Medordi was someone special. We have been together since.

One afternoon, just around that time, I bumped into some guy on the street near my new home. I don't know who he was, but he recognized me.

"Yo, I know you, man. You used to run with the Family."

My body went stiff. I reverted to fight or flight. This could not be happening. I was out. That shit was all behind me like it never happened. Who was this intruder stepping into my new world and threatening my existence? It was a big city, but apparently not big enough.

"Not I, man," I said.

"Nah-ah man. You the guy. I remember you. You that white boy that hung with the bruthahs. Don't worry, we cool man. You was all right!"

For an instant, I slipped back. In my mind I was saying, '*Look here muthah fuckah, I told you, you got the wrong guy. Now back the fuck up off me.*'

But I couldn't say that. I was undercover. I had to take control of my lips. Otherwise, he would know I was bull shitting, and my cover would be blown. What would be the consequences of that? I'm white. That's who I am now. That's who I have to be. I have to be myself.

"I'm sorry, my friend, but you must have mistaken me for someone else."

"Oh. Okay. Sorry man. I thought you were somebody else."

I was.

EPILOGUE

Thumper and Ballah were allegedly selling cocaine. Robazz and Kasseem were apparently dealing in heroin. Each set of brothers had their own crew and there shouldn't have been any problems between them. Pigmy was down with Thumper, and Ballah. LeLe was with Robazz and Kasseem. There was another guy named McGirk. I didn't know him back in the day, but he was originally with Robazz's crew until he started dating Thumper and Ballah's sister. That's when he jumped ship.

Some kind of beef came up between Ballah and LeLe at a club one night and Ballah may have held a grudge. The story I hear was that Robazz and LeLe were shooting pool in a bar near the Bland projects one night when Pigmy came in and told them that Thumper was in some kind of trouble and needed their help at the handball courts in the park. When they got there, they were met by an armed and angry Ballah. Thumper and McGirk were there, and when Pigmy arrived, he joined them. Ballah started accusing Lele of stealing from him, the shit escalated, and Ballah started blasting; first at LeLe, then at Robazz. Robazz literally dove out of his shoes to dodge the barrage, but LeLe caught a life-changing bullet to the spine. He hasn't walked since. Thumper and Ballah were both charged with attempted murder and assault. Thumper did six years and Ballah did twenty-two before being released on parole. McGirk was murdered; apparently stabbed to death. Robazz and Kasseem were charged and convicted for ordering the killing. They got twenty-five to life, running consecutively with another attempted murder charge for Robazz and another murder charge for Kasseem; back to back life sentences for both. As of this writing, they have been in prison for thirty-seven years and they each have another thirteen to do before they are eligible for parole. Thumper and Pigmy are both dead. Jose joined the Marine Corps and became a career military man. He's now retired and living a quiet and solitary life. Pigmy spent half of his life in prison, mostly for burglary. He went in for a few years, came out, got locked up and went back, before he died. I don't know about the others.

A few years back, completely by chance, I met the guy that Kasseem and I tried to rob of his pot when we had Kasseem's nephew in the car. How's that for karma? He was a friend of a friend, and we had been acquainted for about a year before we figured out who we were. That was a tense evening. I apologized sincerely. I had always felt bad about that event. We are still friends and we haven't spoken about the incident again, but he was understandably disturbed when I confirmed what he had in his face that night was a loaded, fully functional 38 caliber revolver.

I contacted the NYC Probation Dept. in an attempt to locate Mr. West. I wrote him a letter and the probation representative sent it to Mr. West's last known address. I was disappointed but not surprised when the email came informing me that the letter had been returned undeliverable.

And then, there's Chenee'. Despite numerous attempts to locate her, I have been unsuccessful. I would just like her to know how grateful I am that she was my close friend during a time when I desperately needed her. Chenee' Gardenhire, without you the thief may never have become the chief.

OCTOBER 15, 1982

I was twenty-five years old and I got the call from the Nassau County PD. The beginning of a grand new adventure. The Police Academy was exciting but intimidating. They tried to get me to quit. They tried to get a lot of people to quit. Some did. I didn't.

My first assignment was the 4th Pct. I drove car 420 in the 0-4 for about five years. The other cops called me "a good cop." They also called me Spike. "Spikes a good cop." Calling a brother officer a good cop is the highest level of praise one cop can give another cop. It meant that I was out there doing my job every day, all day. I decided to go to law school just so I could have something in my pocket for life after 'the job.'

Three weeks before the first day of law school, my CO called me at home. The CO doesn't call you at home unless you're a hero or you're in deep shit. I was no hero. He told me he was sending two guys to narcotics and he wanted to give me a shot. They were forming a new street-level team to deal with the crack epidemic. Narcotics was my dream job. I was trying to get to Narcotics from the day I started. I had to turn it down. You can't go to law school four nights a week and work in Narcotics. Another twist in my tail. What if I had accepted and made the opposite choice?

I was made sergeant after my first promotional exam. It was the one and only time they had essay questions on the sergeant's test. That caused a great turmoil and they scrapped it. I did well. I was placed at number 111. Unfortunately, I didn't have enough time on the job when my number came up, so they passed me by. Luckily, they came back and promoted me once I qualified.

I worked as a patrol supervisor for about two and a half years in the First Precinct with the greatest bunch of guys a man could know. I want to name every one of them, but I know I would leave someone out. Police officer to sergeant is the toughest transition, and I had only about five years on the street. But I was a good cop. My reputation and my nickname preceded me. At my first turn-out, I was introduced as Sergeant Spike. That was a very proud moment.

The itch to go to Narcotics still burned. I did a two-week stint with the narcs on a special training program, with a small select number of bi-lingual officers. I was the only sergeant. Those two weeks were absolutely thrilling. I had to have that job, so I joined "the party", meaning the political party. It doesn't matter which party it was. If you wanted an elite job like narcotics sergeant, you had to have a hook. I didn't have one, but I was going to get one. I worked for the party for about eight months before a spot opened up. One of the three sergeants in Narcotics retired. I made my play. I notified my hook in the party. When the call came from headquarters, the Inspector just said, "Spike, ya got out hooked." That meant somebody else's hook was bigger than mine. Perhaps someone who joined the other party. I wasn't getting the narco job. But the inspector offered me a detective sergeant spot back in the Fourth Squad. I grabbed it. I did not get a warm reception.

The Fourth Squad was crowded with old-time guys. The job was changing. I didn't have a great relationship with the 'dicks' in the Fourth when I was a cop there. Now, Spike was back with about eight years on the job and no experience as a detective. It would be a struggle to earn their respect. Unfortunately, I didn't get a chance. As a result of the incident with Detective X, I didn't stay there long. I was transferred to the Sixth Squad and placed in the fatherly hands of Detective Lieutenant Shaun Spillane. That part of the story has already been told.

I hadn't been particularly interested in another promotion. I was practicing law on the side, I liked my job, and I was still vying for a more invigorating assignment. One afternoon, I was working out in the Sixth Precinct gym with Inspector Mel Kenny. He was the CO of the 0-6. Mel asked me if I was studying, meaning was I preparing for the next promotional exam. I relayed my feelings on the issue and a look of genuine disappointment came over him. He just said, "Oh," and that was it. That bothered me. Mel Kenny was one of the most highly regarded members of our job; by most cops. He did have his detractors. It was said that you were either a 'friend of Mel,' (FOM) or a 'melanoma.' I considered myself a FOM. The respect I had for Inspector Kenny drove me to hit the books. I came out number one on my lieutenant's exam.

I had done about six years in the Sixth squad, affectionately known as ShaunShank when the time came to move on. A few weeks before my promotion, I got a call from Captain Larry Mulvey, which turned out to be a call that permanently altered the course of my police career. Larry offered me the command of a rather unpopular unit called the 'Medical Administration Office' or MAO. MAO was a quasi-internal affairs unit responsible for all the medical and psychological issues affecting department employees sworn and civilian alike. The sweet part about it was that I would keep my detective designation, and I would be in charge. Larry was known as a progressive and innovative boss. Follow the roads that open before you. I accepted the assignment and was promoted to detective lieutenant. By the time I left MAO, mine was one of the most highly sought-after assignments for lieutenants looking for a career path. At MAO, I made my mark as an administrator as I began to learn the principals of good management. I'm quite proud of what I accomplished there and the experience I garnered. Captain Mulvey was a tremendous mentor and a great cop. I took control of MAO and made it into a highly significant force within the Nassau County Police Department.

After about five years at MAO, I came out number two on the captains exam. I got beaten by Bob Turk. Bob and I had a few disagreements before and after we made captain together, but we respected each other. We maintained a good-natured, and spirited, competitive relationship from the time we were patrol supervisors until we both retired as chiefs. When I got promoted, I tried to land the number two spot, the XO in Highway Patrol under the command of Inspector John Sharpe. I had worked for Sharpe in the First. His leadership methods were unorthodox, to say the least, but he was effective. I liked him even though he was a melanoma. Highway cops are a different breed and I wanted to get to know them. I also wanted to learn to ride motorcycles. The job had other plans for me. I stayed on as Detective Captain Spike, CO of MAO. Captain is the highest paid civil service rank. The detective designation earned me even more. And, as the CO of MAO, I would get night differential pay and overtime. I knew that couldn't last.

It was about 10 a.m., one morning in February at MAO, when my boss called me. It was about three months after my promotion to detective captain. By that time Larry Mulvey had also been promoted. For the last eighteen months or so, I had answered directly to Deputy Commissioner Jack Costello. That put me in a highly strategic position. As the CO of MAO, I spoke with the authority of the office of the police commissioner. That felt good. I had juice. And Costello was a cop's cop. That's the greatest compliment a street cop can bestow on a boss. Jack never lost touch with the street. He was the kind of boss that could talk to a subordinate like a colleague without any mistake about his authority, and he would still be the first guy through the door. I really enjoyed working for him. When Commissioner Costello called, he sounded perturbed and that was out of character.

"How do you know Tony Cancellieri," he asked.

"I know he's the new deputy county executive for Public Safety," I said.

Tom Suozzi, a Democrat, had just upset the Republican in the election for county executive. Tom appointed Tony and they had taken over in January.

"Well, he wants to see you across the street right now about working for him. You better get over there."

My mind was racing with exhilaration and trepidation alike. Cancellieri wants me to work for him? I wondered what he could possibly want me to do. I never even met the man. Tony explained to me that they, the new county executive team, were going to overhaul the government operations and he needed someone who knew the lay of the land in terms of the public safety related departments. Deputy County Executive Cancellieri was now in charge of the police, corrections, fire marshall, probation, consumer affairs, and traffic and parking violations. He explained that I would be doing operational audits in every department to find both financial and functional efficiencies. He said he had made some inquiries about me and he wanted to offer me the position. When he told me to take a few days to think it over, I said, "Mr. Cancellieri, the guy who has to think this over is not the man you want for this job. I'm in." I did stipulate, however, that I would not do any work in the Police Dept. Sooner or later, I'd be going back, and I wanted to minimize the number of people there who would have reasons to be pissed off at me. It was a deal, and what a sensational deal it was!

Speaking with the authority of the Office of the County Executive, I now had serious juice. With that kind of authority, I could make things happen. Operational audits were not something I had ever done or studied. Tony assured me that I was capable. Himself a veteran of the NYPD, Tony understood that the police department trains their people to be managers from the day they get to the Police Academy. My transition was seamless, and during my tenure, we accomplished significant improvements. The gravy for me was the opportunity to see behind the doors of West Street, the office of the county seat. The lessons I learned under the tutelage of Anthony Cancellieri were priceless. But after about three years, I yearned to get back to law enforcement. I still loved the job.

When I approached Tony about going back, he asked me for one last "favor." Aside from all the efficiencies we had implemented countywide, the Probation Department remained a challenge. He asked me to take over as Chief of Probation. He said, "I want you to turn that place around." This was unprecedented. Probation is a hybrid department run by the county but regulated by the state. The plan was to allow the director to remain in place but to have him answer to me on a daily basis. I would have to move into an office in Probation and take control. I didn't consider Tony's offer to be an order, but I certainly didn't want to disappoint him. I owed him, and I didn't want to lose his friendship. He was a platinum hook.

As I considered the idea, I recalled that Tony had said, "Chief of Probation." By this time, I had gotten two promotions while working for the county executive: Deputy Inspector and Inspector. This was my shot at earning a star. I agreed to accept the challenge provided for which I would be given three months to prepare. I spent June, July, and August of that year reading everything I could about Probation. The result was not only an education but genuine respect for the critical nature of the work performed by an agency largely neglected. The criminal justice system could not function without Probation. It is an often thankless profession, performed by dedicated officers whose work saves the government hundreds of millions of dollars annually. It also offers low-level criminals opportunities to turn their lives around. This was a concept close to my heart. The Nassau County Probation Dept. was no exception. There I found roughly two hundred professionals anxious to make a difference in society, but they desperately needed direction.

As an outsider, I was not well received at Probation. I knew the director even before I went to work for Cancellieri. He was a good man running an organization based on outdated principals learned from his predecessor. This was his domain and I was an intruder. We disagreed on some significant issues, but he was a team player and a good soldier. In the end, he did the right thing. As far as the rank and file were concerned, they were divided between new school and old school. I had many more supporters among young people than I did with the veterans. You can't please everyone. In an attempt to win some confidence, I held two huge meetings. Every officer had to attend one or the other. The theme of those meetings was simple, "I know nothing about how to do Probation, but I know how to run an organization. I will never tell you how to do Probation, but I intend to make Probation into a respected organization." The meeting got mixed reviews. The County Executive Tom Suozzi, however, was extremely supportive of my efforts. With his assistance, I brought Probation into its own. Barely a week went by when I didn't think about my Probation Officer, Mr. Ed West, and how his wise words brought me to this place. Yet, I dared not speak about it to anyone.

The sense of accomplishment I got from my experience at Probation is indescribable. I had restructured an entire organization. Budget, procedures, training, weapons, grants, labor rules, hiring, Intel; I revamped it all with the assistance of some key individuals in the Probation Department, who were anxious to lead their people into a productive change. After about three years, those individuals were situated in strategic positions and it was time for me to move on. Mission accomplished!

I returned to the police department as the Deputy Chief of the Support Division under the command of Chief George Gudmundsen. George was an amazing administrator. Unfortunately for George, he took the job home with him. Chief Gudmundsen lived and breathed NCPD. He settled for nothing less than one hundred percent from me, and I was up for the task. The Support Division was responsible for the infrastructure of the Police Department. We commanded Communications Bureau, Information Technology, Fleet Maintenance, Building Maintenance, Records Bureau, Police Academy, and Court Liaison. We carried the rest of the job on a tight budget, subject to shifting political priorities. Every day brought a new challenge and that's what made it so much fun. That is also what killed my career.

In Nassau County, we had four departments repairing vehicles: Parks, Police, Public Works, and Corrections. County Executive Suozzi firmly believed that this scenario was creating costly duplication of effort. Back when I was working for his deputy, I was tasked with the consolidation of vehicle maintenance. Consolidation, he said, would create tremendous efficiencies. He was correct, and I set out to accomplish his vision. It quickly became clear that Corrections mechanics would be the most difficult to merge due to prisoner security issues. I tabled that phase and focused on Parks. Parks Fleet Maintenance was the low-hanging fruit. Their work and their job titles were identical to Public Works mechanics. In about six months, I caused them to be folded into the Public Works domain. This resulted in the closure of three garage facilities and an increase in the purchasing power of Public Works. The Police Fleet Maintenance would be far more difficult. They had Police Mechanic titles, the mechanics had police IDs and extra pay, and the operation was run by a police inspector. The Police Fleet Maintenance was the most prestigious garage to work for. No one wanted to see them get absorbed. Lucky thing for me, the Probation Department opportunity came along, and my duties changed. Now that I was back in the PD, County Executive Suozzi resurrected the consolidation project and he tapped me to carry it out. I voiced my disagreement first with the project, and then with the way, I was directed to carry it out. My voice was heard, my recommendations were disregarded, and I was given my orders. The truth is that my loyalty to the Police Department was obstructing my objectivity. But I was a soldier and I was duty-bound to carry out my directive. I did what I had to do, and the consolidation was achieved. Public Works took over the maintenance of the Police fleet.

By the time the consolidation was complete, George Gudmundsen had retired, and I had been promoted to Chief of Support. Super-Chief—three stars! What I failed to notice was that the Police Fleet Service headquarters was located in the legislative district of Nassau County Legislator Edward Mangano. Mangano was a Republican and he was tapped to run against

Suozzi in the next election. In exchange for their support in the upcoming election, Mangano promised the members of the former Police Fleet Service that, if elected, he would reverse the consolidation. Ed Mangano beat Tom Suozzi, and in January of 2010, Mangano was sworn in as the new County Executive. Before the end of March, the campaign promise was fulfilled, and the consolidation was undone. The other shoe dropped in April.

Now I, the orchestrator of the ill-fated fleet consolidation, was once again in charge of the Police Fleet Service. This was an untenable situation. My old friend Larry Mulvey, then in his third year as Police Commissioner, called me to his office for a private meeting. Apparently, the directive had come down from "across the street," that Lowry had to go. The Commissioner told me they wanted to knock me down to captain. This was the typical method used by new administrations when they wanted to persuade a boss to retire. Sworn police brass can't be fired, but they can be demoted back to their highest civil service rank. Captain was a five-rank demotion, and it came with a huge pay cut. I had seen this happen to many before me. Guys would start to feel invincible in those upper ranks. Then they would cry and bitch and moan when they got hit with the captain option. When Suozzi took over, he had cleaned the house in the same way. Three super chiefs got dumped and started a lawsuit. Not me. I knew the game. It was nothing personal, just politics. The day I got my first star was the day I began planning my retirement. But this time, things would be a little different. Commissioner Mulvey told me that he couldn't protect me forever, but he could buy me a few months. As luck would have it, he explained, the county was planning a lucrative retirement incentive for senior employees which would be revealed shortly. He had worked it out with Mangano that I could stick around long enough to be eligible to participate. With twenty-eight years on the job, this would be my golden parachute. The catch was that I had to lose a star. I took it on the chin and shifted my focus to life after Nassau. The only thing that bothered me was that Mangano didn't know me. He didn't know if I was an asset or an anchor. He must have been aware of my dedication because I accomplished the very unpopular fleet consolidation mission. I could have been the greatest police mind of the century and it would not have mattered. I was a Suozzi guy and I had to go.

I spent the next six months re-invigorating my law practice. With an office on the side of my house and a paralegal wife, I had the pieces in place. Retirement parties are the norm in the Police Department, but I declined mine. My career was my celebration; handshakes and plaques didn't mean anything. But my friend Larry Blessinger threw me a demotion party in his cavernous mancave in Garden City. That was an honest event attended by real friends who were snubbing their noses at the system. We still talk about that party every now and then, but it was the unanticipated effect of that party that re-positioned my sails that night, and it came as the result of an innocuous conversation. Larry was a self-made guy who amassed a fortune in the taxi business. We were sharing some laughs over a couple of Cuban cigars when he said, "I heard you're gonna start practicing law again." I told him he was correct. Then he asked me if I wanted to do some subrogation work for him. All I knew about subrogation was the definition, but I accepted the opportunity to learn something new.

Over the next several months, Larry Blessinger taught me everything he knew about third party auto accident claims collection. I caught that ball and ran with it. It didn't take me long to determine that the law practice was limiting my opportunities as I collected multiple taxi, school bus, trucking, and paratransit clients. I incorporated my business and now TranSubro, Inc. operates nationwide. Our success has far surpassed my wildest dreams. What a crazy ride!!!

From right to left: Kendu, Gary, Me, Jose, and CB.